THE SILENT IMMIGRANTS

Table of Contents

THE SILENT IMMIGRANTS

Untold Stories of Courage, Struggles &
Triumphs of West Africans in America

BONIFACE C. NWUGWO, PH.D.

authorHOUSE®

AuthorHouse™
1663 Liberty Drive
Bloomington, IN 47403
www.authorhouse.com
Phone: 1-800-839-8640

Published by AuthorHouse 8/2/2013

ISBN: 978-1-4918-0509-1 (sc)
ISBN: 978-1-4918-0508-4 (hc)
ISBN: 978-1-4918-0510-7 (e)

Library of Congress Control Number: 2013913656

Preface

The ideas for this book have been in my head for over a decade, but it wasn't until five years ago that I resolved to put pencil to paper and jot them down. When I finally decided to examine the stories of West African Immigrants in America, I created a web-based questionnaire for collecting people's stories. Using my own e-mail list of Africans and other email lists of West African organizations that some of my friends provided me, I invited over two hundred immigrants from West Africa to share their experiences about coming to America with me. I made it clear that I was trying to write a book to tell my story and the stories of West African immigrants in the United States. At the end, I received about twenty-three responses each with their own individual story of courage, challenges, struggles and triumphs. I was then faced with the daunting task of picking the sample size for the stories.

Given the number of West African immigrants in America that have stories to tell about their experiences in these United States, trying to limit the number to a manageable size was very agonizing, but I simply had to pick a number. I made the decision to pick four or five individuals in addition to mine and present their stories.

Over the years, I have had several discussions and arguments in various settings with Africans in the United States and have benefited from their comments and criticisms about their American experiences. While the stories of the new generation of African immigrants are vast, they have not yet been told.

This book is an attempt to begin the process of telling our stories by concentrating on the stories of those immigrants from the West African region of the continent. It is my sincere hope that African immigrants, particularly those from West Africa, will gather courage as they did when they left their homelands the first time, and begin documenting their experiences, not just in casual debates and conversations, but on paper, so that the newer generations coming behind them might learn something.

In essence, this book serves as a medium to tell my stories for posterity without having to retell them over and over again. In addition, it is used to present the experiences of other West

African immigrants in America from an African

perspective—four men and a woman—who came to the

United States between 1974 and 2004. It is my

sincere hope that those who read this book would

come to understand the plight of West African

immigrants and why they often do not seek the

limelight when it comes to immigration issues.

Dedication

This book would not have turned out the way it did without the stories I received from so many African immigrants.

I dedicate it to them. To the immigrants and in particular, West African immigrants to the United States that struggle and toil every day to make this country a better place and in the process create better lives for themselves.

Introduction

Watching the recent debates on immigration and the protest marches around the country calling for amnesty for illegal immigrants, mostly from Latin America, one would think that those are the only immigrants to the US. The truth of the matter is that while there are more immigrants, albeit undocumented immigrants who come from the southern borders of the United States, there are also many immigrants that come from across the Atlantic who tend to be silent about immigration matters.

The difference is that almost all immigrants coming across the Atlantic Ocean enter the United States "legally" or documented. Unlike their southern counterparts who can simply walk or run across the border, or tunnel their ways into the United States, those coming across the Atlantic Ocean have to enter through

the proper ports of entry or else they cannot
come in. In other words, they enter the United
States as documented immigrants. It is no
surprise then that West Africans fall into this
category of immigrants as they come across the
Atlantic Ocean.

The media and almost everybody involved in
the immigration debate have successfully managed
to confuse the issue of illegal or undocumented
immigration with documented immigrants whose
legal status may have expired. I will talk more
about this issue later in Part Three. But it is
important to mention that most West Africans
that enter the United States pass through the
proper ports of entry with legitimate papers and
as a result are documented.

Unfortunately, some of them eventually get
caught up with the passage of time and sometimes
they over stay their visas, which then puts them

in the category of "illegal" aliens. However, when their papers expire, they focus mostly on making themselves legal again and as such they never make noise or participate in civil disobedience such as the protest marches of illegal immigrants across the country demanding recognition and a path to citizenship. In most cases, West African immigrants shy away from such public pronouncements because if they do, they would most certainly be rounded up by Immigration authorities and sent "home."

There is no question that West African immigrants do sacrifice a lot and work hard to come to the United States and when they get here, work even harder to make it in this country, but the public seldom hears about them. While a vast majority of West African immigrants are hard-working and law-abiding residents and citizens, oftentimes what makes news is when a

West African immigrant is caught in some illegal act.

For many years, I have been asked in various settings to talk about myself or how and why I came to the United States. Whether it is in a job interview, a social gathering, or in a classroom setting, I have had to tell the same stories, albeit abbreviated versions, time and again. Each time I told my stories and listened to others tell theirs, I noticed certain commonalities in all our experiences. When you listen to these immigrants' stories, you cannot help but feel their courage to venture out of their native motherlands to an unknown world to start life anew. You sense their struggles and the challenges they faced and to some extent, are still facing, and above all, you can see signs of their triumphs as they blend into a society that is far different from what they were used to culturally, socially, and economically.

As I said earlier, there are two main reasons that motivated me to write this book and the first is my children. I wanted them to be able to read these stories and understand how, why, and what I and others like me went through to make it and not to rely solely on oral history that I would have to pass down to them.

The other reason is really to begin to tell our African stories from our own perspectives. While these stories have been limited to a few individuals, it is fair to say that one can easily multiply the number of people whose stories are presented in this book by several thousand times and that is probably how many more who would have similar stories to share.

Another important reason for this book is for the new generation coming behind us. Many of today's youths believe that everything has to be handed down to them on a platter. They just do not want to build the proper foundations for themselves, and yet feel that they can become successes overnight without working hard for it. If this book serves to inspire at least one youth growing up today, then I would have succeeded in my objectives.

While I have used my own name, fictitious names have been used for the other people whose stories are presented in the book to protect their true identities. The book is organized in three parts. Part I presents my personal stories of courage in leaving my native homeland, the struggles and challenges I faced and the rewards of my struggles. Part II presents stories of other West African immigrants' efforts to leave and their struggles as well as their triumphs after they arrived in America. Part III was added to briefly address the West African immigrant in the context of the American immigration debate.

Before proceeding, I'd like to define what I mean by immigrants in this book. As the United States of America (USA) is a nation of immigrants, just saying "immigrants" without being specific confuses the issue. For that reason, "immigrants" in this book refers to the group of West African people that immigrated to America between 1974 and 2004. The US Census Bureau talks about immigration and emigration as components of international migration. Immigration is the migration *to* a country while emigration is migration *from* a country. The US Census Bureau also defines international migration as "any movement across a national border."[1] The crossing of a national border

without going through the proper channel of

entry is what is defined here to be "illegal

immigration."

Based on this definition, there are two

categories of "illegal" immigrants, the first

being those immigrants who entered the United

States without the proper papers. In most cases,

these immigrants did not enter the United States

through the normal ports of entry and as a

result were not documented. Some people

correctly refer to such immigrants as

"undocumented" immigrants. The other category of

"illegal immigrants" is people who overstay

their visas. While their visas may have expired,

they were documented when they entered this

country and as such could be traced if the US

---

[1] U.S. Census Bureau, Population Division 2010. Retrieved October 19, 2010.
www.census.gov/population/www/socdemo/immigration.html

Citizenship and Immigration Services people really want to enforce the law. So whenever illegal immigrants are mentioned in this book, unless otherwise stated, I am referring to "undocumented immigrants".

PART I: RESHAPING DESTINY

Chapter 1:   *Planning My Exit*

"To want to be what one can be is purpose in life."
Cynthia Ozick (*O Magazine, September 2002*)

The Decision to Leave

"Papa, I want to go to the United States to further my studies." That was how I began the conversation that would change my destiny forever. The year was 1979, one late summer day in August, or what Nigerians call the August break, which is the period in the month of August that there is a week or two of break from the relentless torrential rains of the rainy season. One of those weekends, I went home to my village, Alaenyi Ogwa in the Mbaitoli Local Government Area of Imo State Nigeria, which was about 25 kilometers (approximately 16 miles) from Owerri, the nearest city to my town.

I had been employed by First Bank of Nigeria (formerly Standard Bank of Nigeria) since February of that year as a clerk and had been quietly preparing on my own to secure admission from an accredited American university, and obtain a passport and visa to travel to the United States of America.

During one of my frequent weekend trips to the village, I sat down one evening with my father for a family discussion. During our conversation, I mentioned to my father that I would like to travel to the United States to continue my education. "Where would you get the money to go to America for studies?" my father retorted. "Your older brother is already in the US and I still have five of your brothers and sisters in school to worry about. After all, it's only my meager teacher's salary for which the government continues to owe us month-after-month. I simply cannot afford for you to go to the United States of America for studies. I mean, you're lucky and you're at least working for a bank. You will have to take the Joint Admission and Matriculation Board (JAMB) exam and try to secure admission into one of the local universities." My father would not hear of me leaving because as far as he was concerned, it was impossible. But I quietly told him that I had already made up my mind to go to the United States and all I needed from him was to help me get over there and I would take care of myself. I made it clear to him that he wouldn't have to worry about sending money to me for anything as I was prepared to struggle to put myself through college.

I simply could no longer continue to wait for the JAMB, even though working in the bank paid better than the ministries and parastatals (large enterprises owned and run by the state). I did not see banking as a viable career path for my future, although I did not tell my father so, for that would have been foolish as far as he was concerned, since there were many people who would have done anything to secure a job with a bank. With JAMB, there was no guarantee that one would gain admission into a local university, so the only alternative as far I was concerned was to go abroad to America, even though it meant paying up to ten times the amount it would cost to study in Nigeria.

The JAMB (or Joint Admission and Matriculation Board) was created by a presidential decree in 1978 to handle entry examinations into all universities, polytechnics, and colleges of education in Nigeria.[2] The official primary functions of JAMB were to determine matriculation requirements into first degree programs of Nigerian

---

[2]Decree No. 2 of 1978 (amended by Decree No. 33 of 1989) of the Federal Military Government on 13th February, 1978.

universities, conduct a joint matriculation examination for candidates seeking admissions to these institutions, and place suitably qualified candidates in the available spots within the universities. In reality, JAMB was and, in my opinion, still is an official medium for the implementation of a quota system of admission into higher institutions of learning in Nigeria.

Prior to 1978, there were only 13 Federal Universities in Nigeria and each conducted its own entrance examination and admitted its own students.

The military regime at the time setup a commission that concluded that having higher institutions conduct their own admission processes amounted to a lot of wasted resources and unnecessary financial difficulties for the average candidate. In an attempt to address the problem of wasted and uncoordinated resources on the part of higher institutions, alleviate the financial burden for candidates and their families, as well as address what they perceived to be educational inequities in Northern Nigeria, the military leader at the time, General Olusegun Obasanjo, enacted the JAMB decree to implement a system of admission of applicants into Nigerian universities based on a formula that could arguably be called a "state-of-origin university admission quota system."

Under this system, university admission was based on a formula that apportioned admission percentage to prospective candidates partially by merit and largely by state of origin. Specifically, 40 percent of admissions was based on *merit* (i.e., purely on a combination of secondary school examination results and the results of the JAMB's entrance examination to the university); 20 percent was based on

Educationally Disadvantaged Status (i.e.,
applicants from an area historically designated
as having low educational output); 30 percent
was based on what is referred to as *"Catchment
Area"* (i.e., applicants from the immediate
vicinity of the educational facility); and 10
percent was purely by *Discretion*, (a catch-all
phrase for basing admission on the individual
circumstances of the applicant as well as an
allocation for faculty/staff).[3]

In essence, the university admission
formula was instituted to boost the admission
into higher institutions of learning for
Northerners who traditionally had not been
interested in going to school. Standards of
entry into universities was lowered to favor the
Northerners and continued to be lowered, which
arguably has contributed to today's dismal

---

[3] Abdalla Uba Adamu, *Educational Reforms in Nigeria* (Kano: Department of Education, Bayero University,

standard of education in Nigeria's institutions of higher learning.

Suffice it to say that competition to gain admission into universities was fierce, especially for applicants from Imo State (which is one of the states in the Eastern Region of Nigeria), where there were fewer institutions of higher learning. Although Imo State (at the time, Imo State was comprised of the present day Imo, Abia, and Ebonyi States) produced more university candidates and more university graduates than any other state in Nigeria, the State had fewer universities to absorb all those potential candidates coming out of secondary and higher schools. While secondary schools prepared students for the Ordinary Level (O-Level), higher schools were post-secondary institutions that prepared students for Advanced Level (A-

---

1994).

Level), which earned the A-Level students direct entry into universities. In comparison, higher schools then were the equivalent of two-year colleges in America but have since been phased out of the Nigerian educational system. Coming from Eastern Nigeria compounded the problem of admission for me because more than 50 percent of all student applicants for a university admission came from the Eastern region.

The number of admissions was limited and each year, new applicants, freshly out of secondary and higher schools, were added to the pool of eligible candidates for university admission, further diminishing the chances of gaining admission as years passed. Having already spent almost two years waiting for admission, it became clear to me that my best option was to look elsewhere overseas, preferably the United States of America, before it was too late. So, I made up my mind to travel abroad to America even though it would cost a lot more and my parents did not have all the financial resources required to sponsor such a venture.

I graduated from secondary school in 1978 at the age of 18 and it was also that same year that the first JAMB examination was administered. I was one of the aspiring candidates who took the exam that year in April just before my West African School Certificate exam in June, but when the results came out later that year, I was denied admission because my score was a few points below the cut-off point for candidates from Imo state. While my score would have easily secured me a spot if I were from another state outside the eastern region, in my state of origin, Imo State, I was declared ineligible. I had to wait for another

year and try again. Meanwhile, I felt that time
was running out and there was no guarantee that
I would gain admission in my next attempt.

That first year for example, there were
about 19,000 candidates from Imo State alone and
only about 6000 applicants would be admitted.
The following year, more than nineteen thousand
plus the pool from the year before would again
vie for the limited openings into universities.
Given that scenario, it became abundantly clear
to me that I had to seek admission elsewhere
outside the country, but I needed to do
something while waiting and planning my exit. So
I began to look for a job in the financial
sector, government ministries and parastatals.

After several months of searching without
success, my father took me to the neighboring
town of Mbieri to meet his friend whose son was
then the Area Manager of Standard Bank of

Nigeria Limited (now First Bank of Nigeria Limited). A couple of days before we visited the Area Manager, I told my dad that I would like to bring one of my best friends along as both of us had been searching for jobs together and my dad said okay. I spoke to my friend, and he was so excited about the news that he also told his father about it. His father informed my dad that he too would like to accompany us.

On the scheduled date, all of us (myself, my dad, my friend and his dad) visited the Bank's Area Manager, and when all was said and done, he informed us that we would be invited for an interview at the Owerri branch of the bank and we should watch out for their invitation letter. For me, it was a mixed bag of news, I wasn't sure whether to rejoice or cry, but being that I had never held any job before, just the possibility of being interviewed for a job that I dreamt of was very exciting. So I was very grateful to the Area Bank Manager for even promising to invite my friend and me for an interview.

About one month later, I received a letter from the bank inviting me for an interview. My best friend also received a similar letter. We were both so excited about the prospects of a job in the bank that on the day of the interview, we traveled to Owerri very early in the morning, arriving one hour ahead of the time the bank opened its doors to the public. When the bank finally opened, we went in and inquired about the contact we were supposed to meet. When we met the gentleman, instead of an interview as we were expecting, we were told that we would be taking a test along with ten other candidates. Needless to say, we were a bit disappointed, but we gladly took the test.

After the test, I felt a bit disillusioned, so I decided to visit my cousin Innocent Uwandu (now deceased) and his family at Aba (another city in the then Imo State popularly regarded as the commercial center of Imo State at the time) to continue my search for employment. Six weeks passed and there was no news. The second week in February, almost two months after the bank test, I received a message from my father to come home as soon as possible. Unbeknownst to me, a letter had arrived from the bank that week and the letter stated that I should report to work at the Owerri branch of Standard Bank on Monday, February 19, 1979.

However, the message reached me on a Wednesday and the person that gave me the information did not elaborate, instead he said, "your father wants you to come home as soon as possible." Sensing no urgency in the message, I decided to take my time and instead of going to the village the next day or two, I waited until the weekend to go home. I arrived home on Sunday afternoon and my dad handed me the letter from Standard Bank. Upon reading the letter, it dawned on me that I was supposed to report for duty the next day, so I informed my father that I would have to leave that evening. I quickly gathered my belongings and departed for Owerri that same evening. I didn't have any place to stay other than the home of one of my cousins, Mr. Martin Uwandu (of blessed memory), who himself had a large family of eight at the time living in a three-room flat (apartment) right opposite the bank's branch office. Despite the obvious inconvenience to them, he and his wife Amara (also of blessed memory) were happy to receive me and they allowed me to live and attend work from their home. I will forever remain grateful to both of them for their kindness.

Wishes of my Father

There was one thing that my siblings and I had going for us when we were little, we were raised by teachers. In Nigeria, there was a belief that even though teachers were not well-to-do, they always raised brilliant and model kids. So, for many kids whose parents were teachers, there was an unspoken societal pressure on the children to perform. If your parents were teachers, you were expected to be a good student both academically and in behavior.

Although my father was not a wealthy man, he was rich in many ways. As a teacher, his philosophy was simple, "only through education would his family rise above poverty." He believed that whatever level of education he could not attain his children would achieve it for him. For example, in 1973, he was given admission by the Catholic University, Washington DC to study in the United States but had to turn down the admission offer because as his best friend advised him then, if he left, nobody would take care of his children who were at the time beginning to enter secondary schools. When asked about it, he said that his children would do it for him since he couldn't.

One day I had a discussion with my father about the possibility of obtaining university education. He said to me, "while I may not be rich, when it comes to my children's education I will do everything within my power to make sure that they go to school. As long as you are doing well in school and willing to learn, even if it means selling all my ancestral lands, I will do it to send my children to school." At the time, my father was getting ready to construct a new home next to his father's. Although he really needed the new house, I begged him to abandon the project and concentrate on educating us. I promised him then that if he would train me in the university, I would build a new house for him. I must say that he kept his pledge, and I also fulfilled my promise.

In political terms, my father would be labeled a social conservative but fiscally liberal. However, I don't think that labels are enough to describe my father. He is in my opinion the most easy-going and understanding man one could ever ask for as a father. He is a very kind man who took care of his siblings and nine children (two became deceased during the civil war in Nigeria) despite the meager resources he had.

He was not always around when we needed him because he was too busy running around for his community, attending community meetings and functions serving as Master of Ceremonies, Secretary, Vice Chairman or Chairman of each organization or association he belonged to. He began serving his people at a very tender age of 16. He gets along with people of every economic stratum. He associates with the poor, the middle-class and the rich and is never intimidated by any class. While in Teacher Training College, he was the only junior student that could wear traditional suites because at the time he was a Councilor representing my community.

My father always wished better opportunities for us and for people in general. He once explained to me why people say "opportunity knocks only but once". He told me that for one to benefit when opportunity knocks, one has to be prepared, otherwise, opportunity

will come and go and a person will not even know
when it knocks and it will just pass him/her by.
With that word of wisdom from my father, I came
to the realization that I always have to be
prepared just in case opportunity knocks.

A Window of Opportunity

So, on Monday February 19, 1979, I arrived
at the bank all dressed up in slacks and a tie.
I had just turned 19 years old three days prior,
and as I would later learn from one of my
colleagues, I looked too young to be working in
a bank. There were also two other candidates
that reported for duty that same morning. They
were among the candidates that took the test
with me and my friend two months earlier. Two
other candidates had already started work the
month before. It turned out that the bank had
selected the top five of the twelve candidates
who took the test, and I was number three.

Unfortunately, my best friend did not make the list of the top five. After another round of oral questioning that momentous morning of February 19, all three of us were asked to begin our orientation, which lasted a couple of months.

Part of my orientation included two weeks of training in March of 1979 at the Standard Bank Benin Main Branch in Nigeria's ancient kingdom of Benin City, the home of the Oba of Benin. It was during that trip to Benin City that the King of Benin, His Royal Highness, Solomon Akenzua, Oba Erediauwa I was crowned, succeeding his late father, Oba Akenzua II, allowing me a rare opportunity to witness the coronation of an Oba of Benin. As faith would have it, I would come to meet and know one of his sons when I arrived at State University of New York at Brockport.

Getting the job at the bank opened a new window of opportunity for me to pursue my dream of studying abroad. For one thing, I no longer depended on my father to provide me the funds I needed to make certain required preparations to travel to the United States. Those preparations included obtaining a Nigerian passport (at the time, obtaining a passport could take three to six months), securing an admission into an accredited American university, acquiring the suitcases I would eventually need to travel, and obtaining clearance from the student advisory board.

Shortly after I took the job at First Bank, I began working on securing admission to an accredited American university. That job was made a little easier for me because my older brother Dr. Kieran Nwugwo, who had been studying in the States since 1977, sent me a catalog of

American universities. With that catalog, I was able to narrow my search for schools to apply to.

However, after sending out applications to several schools, my brother sent me an application from his school, the State University of New York (SUNY) at Brockport and told me to stop wasting my money in mailing applications overseas. He felt that I should be able to secure admission at SUNY Brockport based on my General Certificate of Education (GCE) Ordinary Level and West African School Certificate (WASC) grade 2 results.

Based on that, I switched gears and focused all my energy and hope of securing admission on SUNY Brockport. Sure enough, in May of 1980, I received a letter of admission and an I-20 form from SUNY Brockport to start in the fall semester (September 5th to be exact) of that same year.

Meeting the Student Advisory Board

In the seventies and early eighties, Nigeria had a Student Advisory Board, which was part of the Federal Ministry of Education. It played a major role in the ability of Nigerians to travel abroad for studies, especially to the United States of America. The Student Advisory Board was created for several reasons, among which were: (1) provide advice to the Nigerian Embassies and High Commissions about Nigerian students and their whereabouts, and (2) provide advice to the embassies of foreign governments on educational qualification and financial ability of Nigerians to travel to those countries for studies.

In a way, the Student Advisory Board served as a clearing house for the foreign embassies,

including the American Embassy. There were many
requirements one had to meet in order to obtain
a visa to travel to the United States. For
people applying for student visas, the
requirements included proof of financial
support, academic qualifications, and
immunizations. Those who were able to
successfully complete the Student Advisory Board
process were issued a sealed letter (more like a
package) for the American Embassy, and one for
the Nigerian Consulate in New York. By receiving
the letter from the Student Advisory Board, the
American Embassy was assured that the applicant
for an F-1 Student Visa had at least met all the
basic paper requirements for a visa.

Usually, when you are admitted to a school
in the United States, the school sends you the
form I-20, which is needed to obtain an F-1
student visa. You are then required to show that

you have sufficient financial resources (such as
family or personal funds, scholarships, loans,
grants, and/or subsidies) available to pay for
your tuition and living expenses. It seemed like
an insurmountable task (at least to me and so
many other students, which is one of the reasons
why too many people did not venture going
abroad), but with due diligence, the
insurmountable task could be made possible, and
I did.

The greatest challenge that I faced was
finding a relative or family friend who would
co-sign with my father as a guarantor. While the
guarantor co-signer was only supposed to act as
a person to vouch for (guarantee) my ability to
pay my way through college, trying to convince
friends and relatives who could co-sign as my
guarantor was like pulling teeth. They were not
supposed to provide any financing whatsoever,

but because it required them to sign an affidavit of support and perhaps provide proof of their assets (such as bank account statements, landed property, or real property assets), nobody wanted to do it. My dad and I visited and begged all the people that we could possibly ask for such favors without success. All my plans appeared hopeless at one point; but when it seemed like I had exhausted all my options, another person from my village who happened to be a good friend of my father's, came to mind. He was no other than the late Chief Emmanuel N. Oguike (Akajiaku I of Ogwa), to whom I will remain eternally grateful.

One day, as we were returning from the house of another relative (who had earlier promised to co-sign as my guarantor, but later reneged), I started thinking of who else we could possibly ask. I then mentioned the name

Chief E.N. Oguike to my father and he said,

"Hmmm that might be a possibility." So we

decided to pay him a visit and it so happened

that he had returned that weekend from Enugu,

where he and his family resided. When my father

and I visited him and explained my dilemma, he

inquired about what it would take. I explained

to him what was required and he quickly agreed

to act as my guarantor. He asked me to come to

Enugu the following Tuesday, and I was extremely

excited.

On the agreed-upon day, I visited him at

Enugu and he drove with me to his bank. He

collected his bank statements, made copies of

titles to some of his landed property and gave

them to me. I thanked him profusely and after

that, my dream of journeying to America was

rekindled again. Still, there were other hurdles

to overcome before appearing in front of the Student Advisory Board.

I still had to get all my immunizations in order and secure my passport. In those days, it was not uncommon for a passport application to take three to six months to be processed. I made contacts for my passport and paid a friend of mine who worked in the passport office the sum of N100 (one hundred naira) for it, although the official fee for a passport at the time was about N20.00 (twenty naira). About two months later, I received my passport. While the processing of my passport was going on, I started my vaccinations. I had to be vaccinated against smallpox, yellow fever, cholera, and typhoid fever. I was issued a yellow International Certificate of Vaccination as proof, which I still maintain to this day.

Armed with the proper documents (including copies of my West African School Certificate (WASC) and GCE O/Level results, my school's Form I-20, course of study, a letter of sponsorship stating name of guarantor, address in Nigeria, statement of financial resources, proof of vaccinations and a valid passport), I was ready to face the Student Advisory Board.

One morning in June 1980, I took off from work, took all my papers and went to the Secretariat for the Ministry of Education at Owerri, where the Student Advisory Board offices were housed. To my greatest amazement, there were more than one hundred students that came for the same reason just like I did. I was told that it was always crowded like that each day the Student Advisory Board office was open. I waited in line for almost two hours, but eventually made my way into the office. The experience was not as bad as I had anticipated. They collected my papers and made copies of each document. I then sat down with another man who asked me a few questions and told me to come back the following week to pick up my letters.

On the appointed date, I went back to the Student Advisory Board office and collected two sealed letters, one for the American Embassy and one for the Nigerian Consulate in New York. The next hurdle was to obtain a student visa from the American Embassy and that meant proving that I had at least one full year of tuition fees and board, a valid passport, proof of immunization, and letters from the Student Advisory Board.

Going for Visa

Having received my clearance papers from the Student Advisory board, the next hurdle was to secure a student visa from the American Embassy. That entailed traveling to Lagos, which

was usually a one day trip by bus from the East.
I quickly called one of my best friends who, at
the time, worked for the British Petroleum (BP)
company in Lagos. He lived with his brother-in-
law and his older sister at the time. I told him
about my plan to visit Lagos for a visa and we
agreed that I would spend the weekend with them.
So I decided to travel on a Thursday afternoon
to arrive in Lagos about 9:00 PM. I had never
visited Lagos before that trip, but I managed to
trace their address that night, arriving at
their residence between 9:30 and 10:00 PM.

When I got to their residence, they were
all sitting outside in their veranda and
enjoying the cool evening breeze. I greeted his
brother-in-law and sister and we chatted for a
while. He then escorted me to his own room for
me to change my clothes. I did not know that he
never informed his sister and brother-in-law

that he would be having a guest that weekend. So while I was getting ready to change my clothes, his brother-in-law walked in and began interrogating me and wanted to know why I was undressing. It was then that my friend intervened and explained to him that I would be spending the weekend with them. He almost chewed off my friend's head for asking me to visit them without his consent. The man had forgotten who I was, but after his wife reminded him of who I was, he apologized. However, as far as I was concerned, the damage was already done. For that reason, I made up my mind to leave the next day after visiting the American Embassy.

Next morning, which was a Friday, I woke up at 5:00 AM and got ready. I wanted to catch the early morning bus to Victoria Island where the American Embassy is, as traffic in Lagos could be a nightmare. My plan was to get to the

Embassy before 7:00 AM to get in line. I
eventually made my way inside the American
Embassy and submitted my particulars, including
my passport.

Before coming, I had used all the money I
saved from my job to purchase a bank draft for
the sum of one thousand six hundred dollars
($1,600.00), which was enough for my first
year's tuition only. After about an hour and a
half of waiting, a lady called my name and I
walked over to the counter. She asked me a few
questions about what I was going to do in
America and I explained to her that I was going
there to study architectural engineering. After
inspecting my Form I-20, and other papers that I
had submitted, she quietly told me that she
could not grant me a visa that day; however, if
I would go back and get additional $3,000 in
bank draft, she would issue me a visa. She wrote

her decision on a post-it note, stuck it in my passport, and handed both the passport and my particulars back to me. I left the American embassy a little disappointed, but more determined. I then visited my friend at his office on Broad Street just to say goodbye. He asked me to stay for the weekend as we had agreed. I declined and gave him a flimsy excuse as to why I had to get back to Owerri, but I could tell that he did not believe that I had to go back to Owerri so soon. Both of us knew that the encounter the night before with his brother-in-law was the main reason, though we did not say it. So I left Lagos for the East that Friday afternoon, arriving the city of Owerri around 11:00 PM.

My plan was to surprise my father, just to prove to him that I meant what I said about going to America, so I accumulated all of those expenses and did all the running around to secure my visa on my own. However, at that moment, it felt like all my efforts and hopes were in vain. Then, out of the blue, something told me that all was not lost yet; after all, the lady at the American Embassy merely said that she would issue me a visa if I came back with an additional three thousand dollars. Just in a flash, my spirits were lifted again and I couldn't wait to get home to bring my father up-to-date on where I was with my plans and what the American Embassy had told me. So I joined the 2:00 PM bus going to Owerri and spent the eight-hour bus ride thinking about how to raise three thousand dollars.

Working in a Bank

After I finished secondary school and was waiting for my West African School Certificate (WASC) results as well as preparing for the

General Certificate of Education (GCE) O/Level exams, I spent a lot of time at Aba with my cousin Innocent Uwandu and his family. At the time, his younger brother, Godspower Uwandu, was working with the then Cooperative Bank of Eastern Nigeria, Aba and it was he who inspired me to dream of someday working for a bank. I developed interest in the bank because of the way bank employees comported themselves.

They were always dressed in suits and ties or slacks with ties. They looked sharp and professional, pure and simple. Banks also paid better compared to ministries, parastatals, and other professions in Nigeria then and they probably still do today. At one point, my cousin Innocent Uwandu sent me to Enugu to meet with one of his friends who was then the Branch Manager of Cooperative Bank of Eastern Nigeria,

Enugu for a possible job interview, but nothing came out of that effort.

I would often fantasize about being employed by a bank and then working in every section of the bank, including entries, cashiering, savings, foreign exchange, and so forth. So when I eventually landed a job in one of Nigeria's top banks, I set out to do just that—learn as much as I could about every aspect of banking. With that goal in mind, I concluded that the best way to learn banking was to simply do it.

Initially, I was assigned to the "Entries" Section, in which the primary duties were mostly clerical in nature. As the name implies, Entries Section was responsible for recording bank transactions in ledgers and attending to customers for clerical matters such as processing of paperwork for bank drafts and bank checks. Very shortly, I learned everything about the Entries Section and became extremely efficient at doing it until it became boring to me. I would migrate from my section to other sections, like the Savings Section, Foreign Exchange Section, or any other section that needed help. I simply volunteered myself to help whenever I finished my tasks. My colleagues and I maintained pending folders, but mine was almost always empty because I strived to quickly finish any assignment that came across my desk so that I could migrate to other sections.

One really needs to understand Nigeria's banking practices during the seventies, eighties, and even up until the mid-nineties to appreciate this story. Everything was manually done, from counting money, to balancing of bank transactions; from recording customer transactions on ledgers to balancing customer ledgers. This entailed using adding machines (the type on which you punch the numbers and pull a lever to record what you have entered) to calculate and balance every ledger on a daily basis. Today of course, most bank transactions are computerized and the people who work in the banks now can perform those tasks with a simple clicking of a button or few keystrokes. Nowadays, even counting of money is a mechanized process.

One important aspect of bankers' activities was the balancing of ledgers at the end of each day and at month-end. This is where 40 to 50 percent of the labor was spent then. For instance, the bank used to open its doors to the public at 8:00 AM and closed at 3:00 PM, but from 3:00 PM until as late as midnight some days, the staff spent their time closing the books. A majority of the book closing process involved balancing the general ledger, entering

customer transactions on their individual

ledgers, and balancing the day's transactions.

All of these were manually done using

typewriters, adding machines, and pencil and

paper.

Every morning before the doors opened to

the general public, the bank performed what was

popularly known as "call over" which was the

pairing of bank staff with the bank's officers

(supervisors, accountant, assistant manager, and

manager) to go over the previous day's

activities by inspecting customer account

ledgers and comparing them with the numbers that

were punched and printed on adding machine

rolls. Using the adding machines' printouts and

the individual account ledgers (usually grouped

alphabetically by last names like A-C, D-E, F-G,

M-N, O-P, etc.), the officers ensured that what

was on the adding machine agreed with the

account holder's balance.

Perhaps it was my curiosity and zeal to

understand the banking process that made me

learn more about banking in a shorter period of

time than did most of the colleagues that

started out with me. One of my specialties was

balancing ledgers. I had the unwelcome

reputation of being able to balance any ledger

that refused to balance. In most cases, it was a

missing penny either in the debit or credit

column of a ledger, or a balance punched

incorrectly that often led to hours and

sometimes days of agony for the person balancing

the ledger. So, word got around even to

management about my special skill.

But it was pure coincidence that landed me

the unique opportunity to do a call over with

the bank managers. It so happened that the bank

manager that arrived about three months after I
started work at First Bank, called me in one
morning to conduct the call over with him. He
and I did it in such a record time that, from
that day forward, he always wanted to do daily
call over with me. So, when he was being
transferred (bank managers usually stayed not
more than six months in any particular branch),
he spoke to the incoming manager about me, who
then continued the practice of using me to do
the morning call over. Subsequent outgoing
managers would talk to the incoming ones and the
practice continued. By the time I left First
Bank eighteen months later, I had worked with
four managers doing morning call overs. The last
manager I worked with, Mr. O.U. Kalu, was so
fond of me that he gave me the nickname "Small
Boy." I didn't mind as long as he was the only
one who called me by that nickname. He trusted

me so much that sometimes he would give me the
keys to the small safe in his office and I never
betrayed his trust.

Doing the Right Thing

During the late seventies and early
eighties, my home state of Imo was going through
a lot of developmental changes as a newly-
created state at the time. Urban renewal,
capital territory construction, and road
constructions were in full gear under the first
and thus far, the only true Executive Governor
of Imo State, the late Chief Samuel Onunaka
Mbakwe, PhD. One of the construction companies
that were building Imo State at the time was a
Fort Worth, Texas-based company named Monier
Construction Company (MCC). MCC did most of its
banking with First Bank of Nigeria and as a
result, their foreman, one Mr. Ray Ennis
frequented the bank almost on a daily basis. The

devil always has ways of tempting us with the
intent of screwing up everything, if you let
him.

One day, Mr. Ray Ennis visited our bank and
forgot his company's seal at the front counter
and I picked it up. With the MCC company seal,
anyone with the proper account number could
withdraw any amount of money from the MCC bank
account. Without it, no MCC checks could be
honored. Keep in mind that about a month
earlier, I had gone to the American Embassy in
Lagos with a $1600.00 bank draft for a student
visa. The $1600.00 was part of the money I had
been saving since I began my employment at the
bank. The American embassy personnel had told me
to go back and get additional $3000 and they
would issue me a visa. So, it was during this
period in my young life that somebody might say
that I got this rare opportunity. As I said

before, the devil never ceases to tempt us one
way or the other.

Immediately after picking up the MCC Seal,
a voice said to me, "Here is your chance to get
the money you need to travel abroad, nobody will
know." But another still small voice said, "It's
not worth it, you do not want anything to impugn
your good name or for anybody to go after your
parents, for that matter, after you leave." It
was that second still, small voice that my soul
wanted to listen to and I did. I went straight
to the bank manager and told him what had
happened. Being that the bank manager had
developed a lot of trust in me, he told me to
keep the Seal as he was certain that Mr. Ray
Ennis would surely return. But I declined to
keep the Seal under my care and instead
requested that he put it in the safe that was

inside his office. He gave me the keys to his safe and asked me to put it in there.

Just about an hour later, I saw Mr. Ray Ennis walk into the bank and his face was almost red and sweaty. I knew exactly why he was there and I called him over. I asked him whether everything was alright, and he confessed to me that he had misplaced his company's Seal and was not sure where he lost it. He wanted to know if anybody in the bank had found the Seal. I told him not to worry, that I picked it up from the counter and that it was with the bank manager. With that good news he let out a big sigh of relief and thanked me profusely. I went over to the manager's office and told him that Mr. Ray Ennis was there for the Seal. The manager opened his safe, took it out and handed it to me to give to Mr. Ennis. It felt so good later knowing that I did the right thing.

My first week at First Bank, Owerri Branch

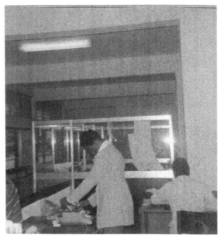

Attending to my Entries duties

Working at one of the Supervisors' desk

At work at the Owerri Branch

At work at the Owerri Branch

Leaving for work while in training at Benin

In training at the First Bank Benin Main Branch with my colleagues

Same party by my bank colleagues just before my departure

At a party by my bank colleagues just before my departure

The Send-Off

The first time I went to the American Embassy in Lagos for a visa was in June of 1980 and I had a bank draft for $1600 payable to the State University of New York (SUNY) at Brockport, but I was told that it was not enough. I was given a condition to go and get an additional $3000 and they would issue me a student visa. So, I had to raise $3000 fast, as I had less than three months to travel since my school would start the first week of September after Labor Day.

When I returned from the American Embassy that first time, I went straight home to see my father. I presented to him everything I had done up to that point in time and what I was told by the embassy. It was at that moment that my father realized how serious I was. When he told me that there was no money to go to the United

States to study he thought it was all over and that I would seek admission in Nigerian universities. Although I did take another JAMB exam and I was successful the second time around, I did not mention it to my father because that would have sealed my chances of going to America for good.

I had gone too far in my quest to go to America that I did not want anything to disrupt my plans. Besides, the admission that I got was to study Metallurgical Engineering at the newly created College of Technology, Owerri. When I registered for the JAMB exam, I selected metallurgy as my second choice, while architecture was my first choice. So I was not very enthusiastic about becoming a metallurgical engineer. For those reasons, I kept the result to myself without telling anybody. I knew that if I told a soul, my father would eventually hear it, thereby destroying my chances of traveling to America. I recall when the results were published in the then Imo State-owned newspaper, "The Statesman," one of my colleagues in the office saw my name and informed me about it, but I quickly told him that it was not me, mainly to prevent any rumors that could eventually reach my father's ears. I never told my father about my admission to the College of Technology, Owerri, but I guess he will know about it now.

Although I did not get a visa on my first attempt and without question I was disappointed, but I was not discouraged. As a matter of fact, I became more determined after my first attempt. At least I knew after my trip to the American Embassy what I needed to do in order to get a visa. All I had to do was come up with additional $3000. So, my father set out to plan a send-off party for me.

In the seventies and early eighties, send-off parties for people traveling abroad to study was in vogue in my part of the country and many people looked forward to it. I know I did because that was one means of raising some funds. In addition, it was a way of informing everybody in town that you were leaving, especially that you were leaving for the United States.

For some inexplicable reason, the people of my kindred (related people of the same ancestry or family) approached my father that they would like to sponsor my send-off party. They offered to take care of all the expenses, but in return, they would get all the revenues realized at the party and would give me the sum of N600 or the equivalent of $1038 at that time. In those days, the Nigerian naira was stronger than the American dollar. In essence, they wanted to use my send-off party as a fundraiser for their association. My father thanked them for their offer, but politely declined the offer. Although my father was not rich, he knew a lot of people, rich and poor. He associated with many people of different economic strata. My father had been attending other people's send-off parties and other occasions in and around my town, and I knew that with his connections we could easily fill up a hall and raise enough money for the $3000 that I needed for my visa. So, I was very ecstatic when he told them no.

With that distraction behind us, my father and I focused on the issue at hand, and that was the planning of my send-off party. We drafted the content of the invitation card with the caption, "B.C. NWUGWO OFF TO USA." We picked a

date in August, specifically the third week, as
that usually coincides with August break. We
made estimates for the send-off party, including
the printing of the invitation cards, the hall,
food, drinks, and the disc jockey. A couple of
weeks later, the invitation cards were out. My
father compiled a list of invitees and
dignitaries for the occasion and the invitations
were mailed and hand-distributed far and near.

Entering my Send-Off reception hall

Engr. S.I. Ibe offering a prayer at my send-off party

Late Mr. I.C. Ukaegbu speaking at my send-off party

Dr. Emma Agwu speaking at my send-off party

Boniface responding to all the advices I received

Toasting the celebrant

Engr S.I. Ibe offering me advice at the send-off party

Late Chief E.N. Oguike offering me his advice during the send-off party

With Friends and relatives at the send-off party

Late F.O. Ihenacho offering me some advice

Posing with my cousins and brother Charles at my send-off party

Fresh out of Secondary (High) School

L-R: my mom, self, sister Margaret, Mrs. Amara & Mr. Martin Uwandu

L-R: My sister Margaret, myself, my cousin Eudora Idemegbulem

L-R: Cousin Martin Uwandu, myself, and cousin Goddy Uwandu

With three of my best friends at the send-off party; L-R: Cy Onuoha, Herbert Achunulo, self and Joshua Ononuju

With my friend, Vincon at Owerri, Imo State

With my Indian friends, Dr. & Mrs. Thalanani at their residence at Awomama, Imo State

Day of departure, wondering about what future will bring in America before leaving home.

Posing with my grandmother, my father's aunties and sisters with my sister
Margaret in the background

On Sunday August 25th 1980, I had my send-off party. Nothing could stop the event that day, not even a torrential rain and I believe God was looking out for me as He had been and continues to do today. That day, the men of my town were holding their town meeting in a different hall at the same venue where my send-off party was about to kick off. Just as they adjourned their meeting, it seemed like the heavens opened up and there was a heavy down pour. That caused all the men who were at the town meeting to run into the hall where my send-off party was going on and the hall practically filled up. By late evening when the event was over, we had raised close to the three thousand dollars that I needed.

The following morning being Monday, I went straight to First Bank of Nigeria Limited Owerri where I worked, and I had one of my colleagues prepare a bank draft for me in the amount of $3000, payable to the State University of New York at Brockport.

While at the bank that morning, word got out to many of my customers that I was leaving for the United States. Before I knew it, those bank customers who knew me and considered me a good worker and a friend made some monetary donations that amounted close to N200. Although I was not expecting the sudden outpouring of affection by those customers, the money came in handy as I used it to purchase a flight ticket to and from Lagos aboard Nigeria Airways.

Getting the Visa

After collecting my bank draft from First Bank of Nigeria, Owerri, I went to the Nigeria Airways office and purchased a round-trip ticket to Lagos via Port Harcourt. I then got in a taxi to Port Harcourt to catch the last flight to

Lagos. I arrived in Lagos around 8:30 pm and caught another taxi to Victoria Island where members of the Nigerian National Assembly resided. I did not know too many people in Lagos that I could go to so I decided to visit one of my cousins, Hon. Barrister E.D.N Uwandu who was at the time, a member of the Federal House of Assembly. Today, he is the traditional ruler ("Eze" or King) of his autonomous community. The other person I could have gone to was my best friend, but based on my last encounter with him and his brother-in-law, I decided not to ask him for a place to stay. So I went to the Honorable E.D.N. Uwandu's residence instead, arriving unannounced at about 9:30 pm. I knocked and introduced myself and explained why I came, and he opened his door and welcomed me in. I was very happy for the way he received me and I will never forget the kind gesture he accorded me.

The next morning, Tuesday, August 26th 1980, I woke up early, got ready and caught a taxi to the American Embassy in Lagos. After a short wait, I was able to submit my papers. About 45 minutes later, I was called to the counter. I went over and it was the same lady that I had spoken to the first time I visited the Embassy. She saw the note she gave me the first time and that jogged her memory. She asked if I brought the additional $3000, and I answered affirmatively. I showed her the two bank drafts, totaling $4600, both made payable to the State University of New York at Brockport. She took the letter from the Student Advisory Board, my passport, and the bank checks and told me to have a seat. About one hour later, my name was called again and I went over to the counter where they handed me my passport with an F-1 student visa stamped on it, my bank drafts, and

another letter for the US Immigrations. Needless
to say, I was elated inside-out, but I managed
to control myself.

When I left the embassy compound, I made
the sign of the cross, leaped up into the air
with joy and shouted, "Yes!" I then stopped a
taxi and headed back to the Hon E.D.N Uwandu's
residence. Unfortunately, by the time I got back
to his residence around 10:30 AM, he had already
left for the National Assembly. He had left me a
note wishing me good luck. Inside the note, he
enclosed the sum of N25. His gift was like a
life saver because other than the N10 I had in
my pocket for taxi, and the $12 (twelve US
dollars) that one of my bank customers gave me,
that N25 was the only money I had on earth. As
luck would have it, pickpockets would steal that
money at the airport, but at the time, it gave
me hope.

After I left Hon E.D.N. Uwandu's residence, I caught a taxi to BP Nigeria Limited on Broad Street, Lagos, where my best friend worked. Having secured a visa with the plan to depart for the United States in a couple of days, if I didn't go over to see him and say goodbye that day, I wouldn't see him again for God knows how long. So, I went to Broad Street to see him and bid him farewell. Unfortunately, when I got to his office, he was not around so I never had the chance to say goodbye after all, but I left him a note that I was leaving for America that Thursday.

As I came out of the BP Building onto Broad Street, I ran into an old friend of mine, another Uwandu. He asked what I was doing in Lagos and I told him that I had just obtained my visa to travel to America and that I would be leaving the country in a couple of days. He was

so happy for me and not knowing how to
congratulate me, dipped his hand into his pocket
and brought out a bundle of Naira (Nigerian
currency) notes. He gave me N10 and although I
was not expecting it, I welcomed it and thanked
him profusely, but I'm sure he did not
understand why I was so grateful. I put that
money in my pant pocket instead of my wallet,
which contained the N25 that Mr. E.D.N. Uwandu
gave me and the $12. I then caught a taxi and
headed to the domestic airport for my flight to
Port Harcourt.

When I arrived at Port Harcourt later that
afternoon, I went to catch the next taxi to
Owerri, but when I reached for my wallet, it was
no longer in my pocket. I checked my passport
which was in my jacket and it was still in
there. I realized then that a pick pocket must
have stolen the wallet at the domestic airport

in Lagos when I was trying to board the plane.
Nigeria Airways had a bad habit of making
passengers walk to the aircraft and struggle to
get in despite that people had their boarding
passes. I did not know that thieves also got in
line, pretending to be passengers and pick
people's pockets during the struggle to get on
board. I thought I would be stuck in Port
Harcourt that evening, but then I remembered the
ten naira that I put in my pant pocket. I dipped
my hand in that pocket and it was still there
and I let out a deep sigh of relief.

I arrived at Owerri late that evening,
about 7:00 pm. And instead of catching the last
bus to my village, I decided to sleep in the
city so as to say goodbye to my friends and
colleagues. They had also staged a little send-
off party for me that Tuesday night, so I had to
attend. The next day, I went home to the

village, arriving at about 4:00 pm. Meanwhile, I
didn't realize that my father was a nervous
wreck at home and waiting for my return. He was
worried sick about the status of my visa
application. When he saw me stroll into our
compound that afternoon, the first expression
that came out of his mouth was, "Did you get
it?" When I answered affirmatively, he leaped
for joy and said, "Glory be to God!" Then I told
him that I got the visa on Tuesday morning, and
I returned to Owerri that Tuesday evening.
However, I stayed back in the city until
Wednesday to say goodbye to my colleagues and
friends. And he asked why I spent all that time
at Owerri before coming home as he was worried
sick about me. I told him that he shouldn't have
worried. I then broke the news to him that I was
also leaving the next day being Thursday August
28, 1980 and he said, "Impossible!" I explained

to him that I had planned it that way because I
needed to arrive at my school before September
1st and he did not argue anymore.

Going to America

Having secured my visa and being poised to
travel to America, there was still one more
thing that was missing, my plane ticket to
America. After all the expenses, I did not have
a penny left, so the N600 needed for my airfare
became the determining factor whether I would
travel or not. Although I did not have the plane
ticket, I did not panic. I told my father that I
needed to get to Owerri early on Thursday
morning, so as to make some arrangements for my
plane ticket. I said my goodbyes to my mother
and siblings who kept chasing our vehicle for
almost half a mile. My father and my older
sister accompanied me to the city and eventually
to the Port Harcourt Airport.

When we got to Owerri, my only hope of flying that day was my good friend Vincent "VINCON" Uwakwe-Uwandu. He had a Honda motorcycle dealership at Owerri and was popularly known by his trade name, VINCON. I explained my situation to him and he volunteered to lend me the N600 I needed, with the understanding that my father would pay back the money in a short time. As it turned out, it took my father almost one year to repay the loan. VINCON is one of those friends to whom I will always be grateful because he came to my aid when I really needed it.

After he lent me the N600 I went straight to the Nigeria Airways office at Owerri and purchased my flight ticket from Port Harcourt to New York. My cousin Martin, his wife Amara, my sister Margaret and my father all accompanied me to Port Harcourt Airport that Thursday afternoon so that I could catch a flight to Lagos. Nigeria

Airways had a direct flight that used to depart

Lagos on Fridays at 11:55 PM and arrived in New

York on Saturday at 6:00 AM, and that was the

flight I needed to catch.

While at the Port Harcourt Airport trying

to check in, my father saw one of our town's

men, Mr. Abijah Ihenacho. Mr. Ihenacho had

returned from Brockport, New York about a week

before and was heading back to America. So my

father simply told me to follow him since I was

also traveling to Brockport, New York. We

reached the Lagos local airport and because the

international airport was a few miles from the

domestic airport, we quickly picked a taxi and

drove to the Murtala Mohammed International

Airport for our flight to New York. We checked

in and the aircraft promptly departed around

mid-night and arrived on time at the JFK

International Airport in New York on Saturday
morning August 30, 1980, a day that will remain
indelible in my memory. August 30, 1980 also
marked the beginning of my struggles and
triumphs in America.

Chapter 2:   *The Struggles to Survive*

"Character cannot be developed in ease and quiet. Only through experience
of trial and suffering can the soul be strengthened, vision cleared,
ambition inspired, and success achieved." Helen Keller

The American Experience

When I left my home country, I was highly
motivated and ready to face hardship, but little
did I know about the realities on the ground
waiting for me when I landed. Coming to America
was a definite eye opener and it quickly became
a clash of cultures, methods, and values. In his
book, "The ABCs of American Culture,"[4] Nussbaum
defined American culture in terms of American
proverbs or what he called "the Ten Commandments
of American culture." While these Ten
Commandments have nothing to do with religion,
they are popular sayings that capture the true
meaning of American culture.

Nussbaum's Ten Commandments also parallel certain Igbo (an ethnic group primarily located in south eastern Nigeria, and also where I come from) proverbs such as "Let the hawk perch, and also let the eagle perch. If one prevents the other from perching, may his wings be broken" ("Live and let live"), "The chicken says that as one scratches, one eats" ("No pain, no gain"), and "When a person falls into a ditch, unless he raises his hands, nobody will come to his rescue" ("God helps those who help themselves").

While there are a lot of commonalities between these American proverbs and African proverbs, I found out that the way they are applied and practiced are sometimes diametrically opposed to each other. To a large extent, my struggles in America could be traced

---

[4] Stan Nussbaum, The ABCs of American Culture: First Steps toward Understanding of the American People through their Common Sayings and *Proverbs* (Colorado Springs, CO: Global Mapping International, 1998).

to those commandments of American culture, especially whenever people contradicted them.

Culture Shock

The first day I arrived in Brockport, New York, some of my brother's friends came to his apartment to welcome me. One of them was a guy from Ghana named Kwashi. He came with his American girlfriend and we all had fun talking about home, drank some beer, and so on. The following week, I was going to downtown Brockport to the post office and I saw Kwashi's girlfriend. I was on one side of the street heading north and she was on the other side in front of Kwashi's apartment and appeared to be heading south. When she saw me, she raised her arm, palm facing down, and made a scratching motion with her fingers. In my culture, that meant come, so I proceeded to cross the street to go and meet her. But as I was crossing the street, she walked away heading south. I couldn't understand why she called me to come over and when I went to meet her, she walked away. So I turned around and headed to the post office where I was going in the first place to get the mail from my brother's mailbox.

After I collected the mail and came out of the post office, I saw Kwashi about 100 feet in front of me. He saw me and made a similar hand gesture like his girlfriend had done earlier. Again I thought that he was calling me, but as I approached him he walked away. I was really upset about what I was experiencing, so when I got home to our apartment (I shared an apartment with my older brother and two other Nigerians), I told my brother what had transpired. He busted out laughing and then told me that in America, when somebody raises his/her arm, palm facing down and making a scratching motion with his/her fingers, that means "hello" or "good-bye."

I suppose culture shock was recognized by the college as a hindrance to progress for international students because one of the courses freshmen students were required to take during their first semester at SUNY Brockport was a liberal arts course called Dimensions of Liberal Education (DLE). Some of the topics covered in that course were cultural differences, or more accurately, what certain gestures (body language, hand gestures), slang, and language mean in the American culture.

On our first day of DLE class, we were asked to introduce ourselves. We were asked to say our names, country of origin, a little background about ourselves including whether we were married, single, or had children or not. When it was my turn to introduce myself, I said everything about me except whether or not I had any children. Since I was not married, I assumed that if I said that I was single it implied no children. When I finished my introduction, one of the girls asked whether I had any children and I said that I was not married. She said, "You don't have to be married to have children." That was another culture shock to me because up until that moment, my cultural upbringing had been that you must be married before you should have children.

The professor who taught the DLE course also served as the student advisor to the freshmen students until they chose their own advisors. The freshmen advisor told us to start thinking about what we wanted to study in school. When I inquired why we should start thinking about what we wanted to do when we already knew why we were there, he said freshmen students really were not expected to know so early in their studies what they wanted to major in. I said that I knew what I wanted to do and what I came to do at Brockport. He asked me to explain what my major would be.

I proceeded to explain to the class that I was offered admission to study architectural engineering, a five-year program that required me to spend three years at the State University of New York (SUNY) at Brockport, studying math. At the end of three years, I would get a degree in mathematics from SUNY Brockport and then transfer to SUNY Buffalo and spend another two years studying architectural design. At the end of the two years, I would receive a bachelor's degree in architectural engineering. It was referred to as the 3+2 year architectural engineering program. The class asked me how I knew that this was what I wanted to do in life and I told them that I made that choice back in secondary school. Then I was asked to explain further what I meant and I proceeded to tell them a little about the educational system of my country.

In the Nigerian educational system at that time, upon the end of class three in secondary school, students were required to choose a minimum of six (up to nine) subjects including English and math. Students then concentrated on those six to nine subjects, for which they had to sit in the West African Examination Council (WAEC) examination for either the West African School Certificate (WASC) and/or the General Certificate of Education Ordinary Level (GCE O/Level). The subjects one specialized in determined the course of study one pursued later in higher institutions of learning. It was a shock to me that college freshmen did not really know what they wanted to do at the outset of college. So coming to terms with the American culture was yet another struggle that West African students including me faced.

It seemed like we had to re-learn US English since most of us were more familiar with British English. After losing points few times in tests for using British spellings, pronunciations, and grammar (American professors felt that our English was too British), one had no choice but to adjust. Some even tried, and I must say, unsuccessfully, to encourage us to change our surnames to our parents' first names, which in most cases are English. The pressure was so strong that some Africans actually changed their names and began answering to their father's first names. If I had done that then, my name would have been Boniface Christian instead of what it is today.

Student Advisor Factor

By the end of my freshman year, I was supposed to have selected an advisor other than the DLE professor who was acting advisor for freshmen. In other to meet that requirement, I chose an advisor from the Math/Computer Science Department at the beginning of my sophomore year. As an international student sponsoring myself through college, I began to think about the five-year program that I was originally working toward.

The year was 1982 and it was the early days of personal computers. I had discussed my concerns about the five-year architectural engineering program versus a four-year program like computer science with my older brother who advised me to look into the possibility of switching to computer science. He advised me to take a course in computer science and see if I would like it. He reasoned that since personal

computing at the time was an emerging field, in

the future that is where the jobs would be. I

gave his advice a lot of thought and decided to

give it a chance, so I registered for my first

course in computers, an introductory course to

Pascal language. It was because of my

consideration of computer science as a major

that I chose an advisor in the

Mathematics/Computer Science Department. It

turned out that my advisor was also the teacher

for the introduction to Pascal, an introductory

computer programming course.

Up until I took the Introduction to Pascal

course, I had never had anything less than a B

grade in any course. When I started college in

Brockport back in 1980, my brother had informed

me that the way to qualify for foreign student

tuition waiver was to maintain at least a 3.25

GPA or better every semester. So, being a self-sponsored foreign student, I was determined to score at least 3.25 GPA every semester so as to qualify, and after my first semester, I was on the dean's list. By the second semester, I was on the dean's honors list because my average GPA was 3.25 or better. So, when I began taking the Introduction to Pascal course, I felt that it was challenging, but nothing that I couldn't handle. By the middle of the semester, I felt that I was doing fine in the course until one day I went to see my advisor for advice on what courses to take the following semester. I honestly knew what courses to take and I had already charted and picked my courses, but since it was a requirement for students to meet with their advisors every semester before pre-registration, I decided to go and see him.

During our discussion, he told me to drop the computer science course and that I should consider another major like business administration. Coming from Nigeria, I thought that the professor's word was non-refutable and students were not supposed to argue with professors even if they disagreed with them. So, after the meeting I simply walked away and swore never to go to him again for advice and I never did. However, I continued to stay in his class, thinking that I would not have any problems, but it seemed like he was out to get me. I was doing fine in my exams, but I felt that he was deliberately giving me low scores in my projects. I refused to drop the course because I knew that I still had a chance to earn a B if I did well in my final project. But, unfortunately, I did not score above a "C" in the final project which ultimately resulted in a grade of D for the course overall, the first time that I had scored anything less than a B in my life.

I was very distraught by his actions because his grade cost me a place on the dean's honors list that semester. I felt very intimidated by him, but at the same time I became more determined to major in computer science. And because I usually get more determined when somebody tells me that I can't do something, I decided to re-take the course that summer, the first and only course that I would take during the summer session. I registered for the course with another professor from India, Dr. Ramasamy Jesuraj. Dr. Raj, as he was popularly known by students, was so impressed with my performance in the class that he enlisted me to help him grade other students' projects. At the end of the course, I earned a grade of A, went on to register for the subsequent courses, and eventually graduated from the Computer Science program with a G.P.A above 3.0.

I still had one more encounter with my advisor before I could graduate. As students were required to get a sign off from their advisors to confirm that they met all requirements, I had to get his signature certifying that I had completed all my requirements for graduation. So, in my last semester, just before the deadline to turn in my intention to graduate to the registrar, I went to his office and sat down with him. Keep in mind that I had avoided him the last two years since I swore never to go to him again for advice. I had my form showing all my courses and he pulled my folder from his cabinet to verify my records (I kept track of my own records).

After going through my file he turned around and said to me, "Boniface you have met all your requirements, you really don't need me." I said to myself, "Of course I don't need you, I am only here for your signature," but I didn't say that aloud. He thought I was there for some advice, but I simply told him that I needed his signature so that I could graduate. He signed my form and I walked out of his office, never to see him again.

The experience with my academic advisor made my life a living hell for just one semester I took his class. It felt as though he was trying to steer me away from studying computer science for reasons I didn't understand, and didn't care to know. Needless to say that I did graduate with a degree in computer science and went on to obtain two master's degrees, one in information management systems from SUNY

Brockport, and another in software development and management from Rochester Institute of Technology, and subsequently a doctorate degree in information technology management. If I had listened to him at my early stages of my introduction to computers, I probably wouldn't be doing what I am doing today.

Sophomore year at SUNY Brockport

Senior year at SUNY Brockport

SUNY Brockport Graduation Day Procession

Graduation Day from SUNY Brockport with my brother Dr. Kieran Nwugwo

BS Graduation Day, SUNY Brockport   BS Graduation Day, SUNY Brockport

With my three SUNY Brockport supervisors at Jeff's wedding. L-R: Boniface,
Bob Giacomo, Jeff Love and Nelson Brown

Using Soccer as Therapy for Loneliness

Nothing reminds international students about their foreignness than long breaks (winter, spring and summer breaks). During the long breaks, SUNY Brockport campus and the village in general often felt like a ghost town. After students go home, one would wake up the next day and all of a sudden, everywhere would seem deserted and quiet. In Brockport, when the spring or summer breaks loomed, it always brought great expectations for most students. Who doesn't like spring break or summer vacation? Just the thought conjures up images of sticking ones feet in the sand, playing in the street, getting a summer job and making some money. But it was not for everyone, especially African students.

The harsh reality for most of the West African students was that summer vacations were nothing more than idle time, the season when foreign students were left to mope around because they could not afford to go home and they were not allowed to work outside of the College campus as their student visas did not permit them to work. Long breaks were often the period of boredom and brain freeze for most African students.

For several years, it was the case with many of us. Although some of us had campus jobs, and also would go to local farms to pick apples, cabbages, grapes and other produce, at the end of the day, we still did not have other exciting ways to spend our long summer holidays.

During my first summer vacation in Brockport, I purchased a soccer ball and in the evenings I would go to the Brockport High School soccer field and kick some balls around. Word got around to the African students and every evening many of them would come out to play soccer. We formed a rag tag team of international players. We had players from all over the world - Nigeria, Ghana, Liberia, Cameroon, Angola, Ethiopia, Eritrea, South Africa, Tanzania, Venezuela, Mexico, Haiti, Jamaica, Trinidad & Tobago, United Kingdom and the United States. We continued playing every summer until the summer of 1986 when one of our players arranged a friendly match with the Jamaican team that used to be the champions of the Premier Division of the Rochester & District Soccer League (RDSL), which was part of the Northwest New York Soccer Association.

By the end of that friendly match, we had defeated the RDSL Premier Division champions 2 goals to 1. The officiating referees of the game were so impressed with us that they encouraged us to join the league.

At the RDSL end of season meeting that year, one of our players, attended the meeting at the invitation of one of those referees and petitioned for admission to the league. The referee provided the recommendation for us and testified that we were a very good and organized team. The league voted to admit us into the league starting from the 5th division where every new team always started and worked their way up the league's division hierarchy. When our player was asked for the name of the team, he didn't know what name to give but when pressed to give a name, he said, "Rochester-Nigerian Soccer Team" and the name stuck. So in the 1987 RDSL season, Rochester-Nigerian Soccer Team made its debut in the 5th Division. We played in the league for 7-8 years advancing through the divisions up to Division 1. The team won the Division 4 Championship and was runners up for

Division 5 and Division 3 and was even relegated one season from Division 3 to 4. The team stayed together with the league until 1994 when I left Rochester.

As the Team's Coordinator and with nobody else willing to step in, coupled with the fact that many players started relocating to other parts of the country and yes, the players were also getting older, the team struggled for one more season and after the 1995 season, another group took it over and renamed the team. That ragtag team that eventually organized under RDSL to a large extent was very therapeutic for many West Africans in dealing with boredom and loneliness.

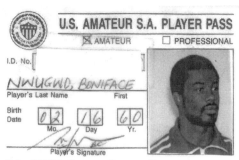

My RDSL Soccer Season Pass

Soccer Playing Days in Rochester

Rochester-Nigerian Team 1987

Rochester-Nigerian Team 1988, getting ready for the game to start

The 1989 Rochester-Nigerian Team

The 1990 Rochester-Nigerian Team

The 1990 Rochester-Nigerian Full Team

The 1991 Rochester-Nigerian Team

Discussing the progress of the game at the half with one of the players

The 1992 Rochester-Nigerian Team

One of our victory celebrations after winning the game and the Championship

Posing with our trophies with Dan Ajegba, one of the team's MVPs

Racism in the Church

I have had a few African-American friends ask me about my experiences with racism in America. I always tell them that I have not experienced racism. That is not to say that it does not exist or that I have not actually experienced it, just that I refuse to let it bother me. However, when pushed to assess my experiences, I narrate stories about my encounters and simply let the listeners draw their own conclusions, stories such as my experiences in the church.

I was born and raised a Roman Catholic and, as far as I can remember, I have always attended mass almost every Sunday. When I arrived in Brockport, New York, I was happy to see a Catholic church on campus, the Newman Oratory. Although the main Catholic Church was on Main

Street in downtown Brockport, my brother and I preferred to attend the one on campus partly because it was closer to our apartment and partly because it catered to college students. I was surprised to observe what some might regard as discriminatory practices amongst the congregation, which were predominantly white students, college professors, and their families.

On my first day at the church, my brother and I arrived early and took our seats in one of the pews. Being one of the first to arrive, I observed that as the congregation arrived and took their seats, our row remained empty as it appeared that nobody wanted to seat near us. It was only after all the seats were taken that people started to sit down in the pew we were sitting in. This happened again the following week and I began to doubt that I was dealing with Christians. I decided to stop going to church, so I skipped one week. However, I felt so bad not attending Mass that the following week I went to the Catholic Church on Main Street, but my experience was no different. I decided not to attend Mass anymore until I went back home, just as many West African students had done.

But after a couple of weeks of not going to church, I resolved that I would continue to attend Mass regardless of what happened. I came to the conclusion that after all it was not human beings that I was worshipping, rather, the Lord Jesus Christ. I simply changed the time that I arrived in church and arrived a little late after almost every seat had been taken. I would then squeeze my way through people to sit down wherever there was space. I reasoned that if I ever sat down and people didn't like that I was sitting next to them, they could get up and leave if they wanted to, but none ever did. From that point on, I never missed another Mass again and resolved to handle the behavior my own way. Was it prejudice or racism? You draw your own conclusion, but I know that for a while, I felt very uncomfortable attending Mass every week at the Newman Oratory.

Studying in Tears

While running into people like my undergraduate academic advisor was an unwelcome struggle, some of my biggest struggles were about my ability to pay my way through college and still eat and pay my rent. After I arrived at SUNY Brockport, I paid off one full year of tuition with the hope of securing some on-campus temporary job to supplement whatever I had left. My brother had already advised me to strive for A's and B's in my courses as that could help me

qualify for foreign student tuition waivers.
When I started college in 1980, President Jimmy
Carter was still in office, but in a heated
election campaign against the quondam Governor
of California, Mr. Ronald Reagan, who would
eventually unseat him. President Carter's
educational policies made it possible for
foreign students to receive some tuition
assistance in the form of tuition waivers based
on need for those students who maintained at
least a GPA average of 3.25 or higher.

After my first year, I applied for the
foreign student tuition waiver and, because I
had maintained a 3.25 GPA average or better and
was in real need to pay my tuition, I was
granted a tuition waiver, thanks to the then
SUNY Brockport foreign Student Advisor, the late
Roy Agte. I received tuition waivers for two
semesters until the Reagan administration

settled in. President Reagan then cut the education budget so drastically that the tuition waiver was eliminated.

When the tuition waiver was scrapped, it signaled the beginning of my major problem for the next two years, and that was how to stay registered as a full-time student so as to remain legal according to the immigration laws. Any semester that a foreign student failed to register for a full-time load, the student's name was supposed to be sent to the Immigration & Naturalization Services (INS) and the INS was expected to commence deportation proceedings. So, I tried not to create any immigration problems by doing everything possible to be on full-time student status.

I had landed a temporary job with the college's Shipping & Receiving Department early in November of 1980, a place that I would come

to work for the full four years I spent in
Brockport. I was introduced to Dr. Ed Kumar by a
cousin of mine, Dr. Gervase Eleonu, who at the
time, was completing his doctorate program at
the SUNY Buffalo. Dr. Ed Kumar was his classmate
at SUNY Buffalo and at the same time, the
Comptroller of SUNY Brockport. Dr. Ed Kumar had
come to learn a lot about Nigeria through his
interactions with Dr. Gervase Eleonu and other
Nigerians and he knew that economic conditions
were worsening in Nigeria by the early eighties,
as students were having problems receiving money
from home. Foreign exchange was drying up and
Nigerian students' debts to schools were
beginning to mount as most of them were no
longer receiving remittances (or scholarship
funds for those who were on scholarship) from
home.

So when I went to Dr. Ed Kumar's office seeking for a temp job, he knew exactly what my situation was. He gave me a note and sent me to another guy by the name of William "Bill" Benz, who was the overall supervisor for the college's Shipping & Receiving department. Bill gave me a job and sent me to the shipping and receiving dock to meet the three supervisors that were practically in charge of shipping and receiving for the college: Nelson Brown (son of the former president of SUNY Brockport, Dr. Albert Brown), Jeff Love, and Robert Giacomo (who at the time was also a captain in the United States Army Reserves). I would come to build a solid working relationship with these three gentlemen. They refused to let me go and so they did everything within their power to ensure that I continued to work in that department until I graduated from college.

Whenever my temp funds were exhausted, Bill would inform Dr. Ed Kumar, who would then transfer funds from his own budget to the temp account so that I could be paid. I worked 20 hours a week, but any time there was a holiday, I would automatically increase my hours to 40 hours a week and my three supervisors loved me for that. They didn't know that I looked forward to working more hours because I needed the money. My life simply revolved around work and classrooms as I would go to class and then from classroom to work and back to class again.

After the tuition waiver was taken away, I had to struggle to pay my tuition, pay my rent, and at the same time, feed myself. It got harder and harder every month that I started missing some tuition payments and as a result, would owe the school at the end of each semester. My feeding amounted to two meals a day: lunch and dinner. I reached my lowest point when I went to register one semester and the Bursar refused to allow me to pre-register because at the time I still owed the school about $600 from the previous semester. I knew that if I didn't register, my name would be sent to the INS and my problems would be exacerbated.

So I went to Dr. Ed Kumar, who was also the Bursar's boss. I explained my situation and told him that I had promised to be paying my tuition in installments so that by the end of each semester, I would have finished payment, however, the Bursar refused. But Dr. Ed Kumar, knowing my unique situation because of problems back home, agreed to put me on a payment plan.

Although Nigerian students' problems were mounting because the Nigerian military regime was no longer allowing remittances overseas, my true situation was that there wasn't any money coming from anywhere. Only my brother and I knew that and Dr. Ed Kumar did not. So, I made a pact with Dr. Ed Kumar that as long as I finished paying my tuition by the beginning of each semester, he would give me an authorization letter to register for another semester. I agreed to the plan and worked hard to keep my end of the bargain even if it meant eating just once a day so as to save money to pay for my tuition. Whenever it got really bad, my brother who was at the time a graduate student at SUNY Buffalo would sacrifice $200 - $300 from his student loan and send to me to help pay my tuition. I must say that Dr. Ed Kumar also kept his own end of the bargain, and I will remain eternally grateful to both of them.

It was basically studying in tears, pure and simple, but that was how I eventually completed my college education, even though the

Bursar was totally against it. It seemed like the Bursar did not like me for some reason, but it didn't bother me even one bit. By the time I graduated in May of 1984, I owed the school only $800, with no student loans or any other financial obligations to anybody.

Working the Farms

After Congress passed the Immigration Reform and Control Act (IRCA) of 1986, which gave amnesty to all illegal aliens who were working illegally in agriculture, many West African students came forward and applied for permanent resident status based on the fact that they worked illegally in agriculture. The Immigration Services thought that they were lying. While some who did not work in the farm may have tried to use the opportunity to obtain green cards, the truth of the matter is that the vast majority of Africans that came forth did work in agriculture, albeit illegally.

I know for a fact that many West African students, myself included, used to go to the farms during the summer seasons and help the farmers pick apples, cherries, cabbage, etc. We were only working in the agriculture business during the summer months, particularly on weekends, to supplement our food budgets. Those who did not have on-campus summer jobs worked in the farms daily and others went to the farms in the late afternoons after they came back from their on-campus summer jobs. It was not uncommon for us to be paid $20 to $40 each day. This money came in handy for groceries. So, when the IRCA was passed in 1986, many of us came forward, although many of our American friends could hardly believe that we were going to school, doing our campus jobs, and at the same time, working on the farms.

Even some of the farmers tended to forget who worked and who did not work because they paid the student farm workers under the table. However, those who had good documentation, such as pictures that were taken at the farms with other workers when they were working, or with the farm owners' family members, their pets, or the farmers themselves, were easily provided clearance papers by the farm owners. Little did we know that the pictures we were taking as souvenirs to remind us about what we went through when we were in college would a few years later help us change our immigration status. For me, though I was qualified to take advantage of the 1986 IRCA amnesty, I did not use it because I was already married to a United

States citizen at the time and had changed my status a year before through my marriage.

Denial to Join the Navy

While studying at SUNY Brockport, I harbored a secret ambition to become a US Navy pilot. My biggest challenge was how to join the Navy. SUNY Brockport had an Army ROTC program, but not the Navy ROTC, so I never approached the Army ROTC to inquire about my qualifications. In my junior year of college, I wrote the Navy requesting information on how to join. They sent me some application forms, which I completed and sent back. I was eventually informed that I did not qualify to join the Navy because I was neither a permanent resident nor a citizen of the United States at the time. I was, of course, disappointed as my dream of becoming a Navy pilot would never materialize. But sometime in 1984 just after my graduation, I received a letter from the Navy and I thought that they had changed their mind. It turned out to be an invitation for me to visit the USS Stark, which was going to be at the Port of Oswego in Upstate New York during one of the summer months. I misplaced the letter and did not find it until few days before it was scheduled to leave Oswego.

When I finally found the letter, I decided to drive to Oswego from Brockport since I still had a couple of days left. When I got to port of Oswego, I did not see anything resembling a Navy ship. I inquired about the ship and was told that the Stark had sailed the day before. The USS Stark had left the port of Oswego two days earlier than scheduled because they were ordered to head to the Persian Gulf. It was during the Iran-Iraq war and the ship was ordered to join other ships that escorted oil tankers through

the Persian Gulf and the Straits of Hormuz. In
1987, an Iraqi pilot flying the F-1 Mirage
aircraft launched two French-made *Exocet*
missiles at the Stark, killing 37 sailors and
wounding 21 others. When I heard the news, I was
personally distraught over the loss of the
sailors because I felt that if I had been to
Oswego three days earlier in 1984, perhaps I
could have met some of them in person.

After I was denied the possibility of
joining the Navy in 1984, I made another attempt
again in the early nineties to join either the
Air Force Reserves or the Marine Reserves.
Again, I was turned down. This time, the Air
Force denied me because of my vision because by
then I had started wearing corrective lenses.
And the US Marines turned me down because I was
then 39 years old and was considered too old.

Perhaps it was my interest in the military that made it easier for me to allow my youngest brother to join the Marines in 1992. Not too long after my siblings immigrated to the United States in 1991, my youngest brother, who was eighteen when he arrived, received the Selective Service notification. He filled out the form and sent it back. By 1992, he was approached by the US Marine Corps recruiting agents. At the time, he was just completing his freshman year in college. As his guardian at the time, I had considerable influence on what he did. He and I sat down one day and talked it over. We discussed the pros and cons and I convinced him that the Marine Corps would make him a man as well as help him build character.

He enlisted with the Marines and went on to Parris Island, South Carolina for boot camp. Just a couple of weeks before his graduation, he suffered a compound fracture in his leg and could not graduate with his class. He insisted on continuing and had to spend another three months in boot camp with another platoon. He went on to serve in the Marines for four years of active duty and another six years as a reservist.

Changing Immigration Status

After my graduation from college in May 1984, I decided to exercise one option that the INS used to provide to foreign students who studied in the United States, and that was a one-year period of practical training experience. In order to work, I needed to find a job, but I could not find a job without my official college transcripts. (Recall that I still owed the school the sum of $800 when I graduated.) For that reason, the Registrar refused to give me a copy of my transcripts so that I could look for a job. It became a "Catch-22"[5] type of problem. I was owing the school and I wanted to pay it off so that I could get my transcripts and diploma, but in order to pay, I had to get a job, but I couldn't get a job because I didn't have my transcripts. So I went back to my trusted friend Dr. Ed Kumar, the comptroller, who understood my dilemma better than his subordinates.

I explained my dilemma to Dr. Ed Kumar and what I needed to do and again, he gave me a letter for the Registrar to release a copy of my transcripts so that I could use it to find a job. By September 1984, I enrolled with some placement agencies to find me temporary assignments and by the second week of September, I started taking job assignments in Rochester, from light-industrial assignments to financial

---

[5] Heller, Joseph. *Catch-22*. New York: Simon & Schuster Publishers, 1994

accounting jobs, to data entry positions; it didn't matter to me what it was. My plan was to work for one full year, complete a master's degree program within that period and then go back to Nigeria. As a consolation for coming to America and paying ten times what it costs in Nigeria, one was expected to complete at least a master's degree before heading back.

However, it was during the first six months of my practical training that my first wife was introduced to me by a mutual friend who knew her through his own girlfriend. Within a couple of months, we started talking about marriage and by the end of 1984, we became husband and wife, a relationship that would last eight years.

Based on the fact that I was married, I moved from Brockport, New York to the city of Rochester, New York and in January of 1985, my wife filed a petition to adjust my status. By

March of 1985, the INS called us for an interview and consequently changed my status to permanent resident. Everything went very smoothly, so it seemed until I decided to visit Nigeria in December of 1986. It had been more than six years since I left home, so I wanted to visit and see my parents, siblings, and other members of my family that I had not seen in over six years.

On my way back from that trip in early January of 1987, through the JFK port of entry, the INS lady looked at me and said, "Do you have a 21-year old child in this country?" and I answered no. She said, "I didn't think so as you're only 26 years old". I asked her if there was any problem and she said no, only that somebody at the INS had made a mistake and coded my green card as if I had a 21-year-old child. She then gave me a form and circled an INS address to send it. She told me to fill in the form, mail it to the circled address, and the mistake would be corrected. So I went home to Rochester, filled the form and sent it out. That was the beginning of what became a nightmare for me and a struggle with the INS that would take more than two years to resolve.

Nine months after I sent in the form to correct the mistake on my green card, I still had not received any acknowledgment from the INS about when I would receive a replacement card. I decided to go to their Rochester office to make some inquiries. I gave the INS person my information and she called their Buffalo office. She was placed on hold for a long time, and finally somebody got back to her that they were looking for my file. She told me to come back the following week and she would have some information for me. The following week I went back, and there was still no news.

The reason they could not find my file was because they had moved my file to another location that was preparing deportation proceedings against me. After a few more weeks, I finally received a letter from the INS informing me that my adjustment was made in error because my US citizen spouse who had petitioned on my behalf was still married to somebody else, and as a result, they would rescind my status and deport me from the country. When I read that letter, I said no, that could not be the case. I thought that perhaps somebody was playing a prank, but I knew it was not a prank. So I contacted a lawyer; meanwhile, I asked my wife about what the INS was alleging.

My wife then told me that she was once married to a Muslim man in 1975, when she was very young. She said that both the wedding and the divorce were handled the traditional Muslim way and as a result, she didn't think anything of it. It was after I received the INS letter that she said that she had mentioned her Muslim marriage to the INS officer during her interview and had actually shown him a copy of her marriage certificate, which I did not know existed. The examiner had made a copy of the marriage certificate and placed it in my file, however, he did not ask her for the corresponding divorce certificate and she did not provide him with it. So, unbeknownst to me, this marriage certificate was lying in my file without a corresponding divorce certificate, so when I sent in my form to correct the mistake on my green card, the INS reviewed my file and found her first marriage certificate and my marriage certificate but no corresponding divorce certificate for her first marriage.

We both met with a lawyer who asked her some questions about the marriage and what had happened. I then told the lawyer that I had done nothing wrong and there was no way I would agree to what the INS was suggesting and I became determined to fight it. My lawyer made attempts to contact the mosque in New Jersey where the marriage and divorce took place and made several attempts to contact the Imam without success. They refused to help us answer certain questions and would not cooperate with the lawyer. My lawyer asked us to contact them on our own to see if we would be lucky and we did, but they still refused to cooperate. This went on for almost nine months and we were getting nowhere, meanwhile, my legal bills were mounting. My lawyer then suggested that he would go ahead and file for another divorce to terminate my wife's first marriage and after that, she and I should remarry and start all over again.

While this was going on, the 1986 IRCA or amnesty program was also in full gear, and some people suggested that I should use the amnesty program to change my status rather than face deportation. But I was determined to fight it out with the INS because I felt that I had done nothing wrong, so I chose not to take advantage of the 1986 amnesty program, even though I was qualified for it. Eventually, I reluctantly took my lawyer's advice, paid for the divorce and he processed the formal divorce to counter the marriage certificate the INS had placed in my file. We then remarried and my wife filed a new petition to change my status.

The INS examiner handling my case tried to make a deal with my lawyer after my lawyer convinced him that I did nothing wrong and that the marriage which my wife had entered into with a Muslim man in 1975 was duly terminated, even though she didn't have the proper papers to prove it. The INS examiner offered to rescind my green card and allow my wife to file a new petition on my behalf. I felt that it was basically a punishment that I did not deserve; however, I informed my lawyer that the only way I would agree to such an arrangement was if the INS would give me another interview the same day they rescinded my green card. In other words, they would have to process me for a new permanent resident status immediately after rescinding my old one because I did not want to be out of status even for an hour.

The INS examiner agreed and my lawyer relayed the message to me. A few weeks later, I received a letter from the INS to appear in Buffalo for the rescission of my permanent status and at the same time, for a new status adjustment interview. My spouse and I appeared before the INS in Buffalo and they rescinded my first permanent residence status, granted me another interview and approved me for a new permanent resident status the same day. I still did not understand what the point was in making me go through the whole process again other than pure bureaucracy. But that period between January 1987 and May 1989 when it was finally settled, was probably the worst period of my entire American experience. Unfortunately, that whole experience affected the relationship with my wife and in 1993, the marriage ended amicably in a divorce.

Corporate Ceiling

Whether people believe it or not, there exists a real glass ceiling for women and minorities in this country, as confirmed by the Glass Ceiling Initiative report issued by Labor Secretary Lynn Martin in 1994.[6] In praising that report, former Senator Bob Dole described the glass ceiling as "invisible, artificial barriers blocking women and minorities from advancing up the corporate ladder to management and executive level positions".[7] While it is bad enough for women and minorities, it is even worse for African immigrants who, in addition to all the factors that lead corporations to have glass ceilings, have to battle with what some call "deep accents." In the corporate world, this factor is coded as a communications challenge.

---

[4] U.S. Department of Labor. (1991). *A Report on the Glass Ceiling Initiative.* Washington, D.C.
[7] Glass Ceiling Commission, Good for business: Making Full Use of the Nation's Human Capital. A Fact-Finding Report of the Federal. Glass: Ceiling Commission (Washington, D.C.: Robert B. Reich et al, 1995).

First of all, I did not get my corporate job following the more traditional way in which after graduation from college, you apply for jobs, attend interviews, and eventually land an entry-level position with a company, and then gain some experience on the job. While most of my graduating class of 1984, especially those who graduated from the computer science program, secured job offers through the traditional method as I described above, I came in through the back door.

After graduation, I had to go through placement agencies to find temporary assignments. After several months of going from one temporary assignment to another, I was sent to help out in the accounting department of one small company, Merkel-Donohue, Inc. in Rochester. They decided to offer me a job to run their data processing department and become their resident programmer. That was my first break in obtaining a real job in the corporate world. I spent four years at Merkel-Donohue. After completing my first graduate program and while pursuing another master's degree in software development and management from the Rochester Institute of Technology, I was offered a position at Eastman Kodak Company as a software engineer. So, by the time I landed the job I was looking for, most of my classmates had already had four years of experience and seniority at Kodak.

At Merkel-Donohue as Data Processing Coordinator

At Merkel-Donohue as Data Processing Coordinator

At Merkel-Donohue as Programmer Analyst

At Merkel-Donohue, troubleshooting a user's computer problem

Service At Merkel-Donohue as Programmer Analyst

Service At Merkel-Donohue as System Operator

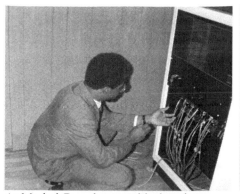

At Merkel-Donohue troubleshooting a system problem in the computer room

At Merkel-Donohue troubleshooting a line printer problem

At Merkel-Donohue going in to the computer room

At Merkel-Donohue, getting ready for system backup at the end of the day

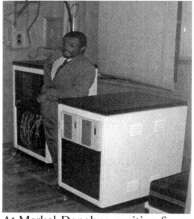

At Merkel-Donohue, waiting for system backup to complete

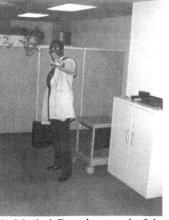

At Merkel-Donohue, end of the day, time to head to school

Now, having landed a job in a big corporation, I thought advancement would be faster. Perhaps I was naive at the time, but I thought that if I worked hard and hung in there, acquired the necessary background and training, then eventually, I'd be recognized for my efforts and rewarded with advancement. But as I would come to find out, there were truly other forces at work that prevented minorities and women from advancing. For a West African immigrant in a big multinational corporation like Kodak, all of those forces plus some more are always in effect. The first excuse is usually that there are not enough qualified women and minority candidates available. This was one of the reasons why I made sure that I obtained advanced degrees and other training to counter this lame excuse. Another excuse often used is communications.

When educational qualification was no longer the issue, it seemed like they found other excuses. For Africans, the code word was communications. What I couldn't understand was how people from European countries other than Great Britain or people from Latin America and Asia (who by the way speak English as a second language) could be understood, but West African immigrants, who in most cases use English as their official language, cannot be understood. It seems that there is indeed a concerted yet subtle effort to make sure that Africans do not move up the corporate ladder, no matter what. End-of-year performance evaluations are often used as the mechanism to keep people down and despite whether every year you receive accolades and adulations for what you did the year before, communication is still identified as one area needing improvement. When you ask what they mean by "communication," nobody will give you a definitive answer. Yet another excuse is inexperience.

No matter what you do, there is always the possibility that you won't know everything you're supposed to do about a new position until you begin handling the responsibilities of that position. While management would always give a White person an opportunity to learn on the job, for minorities and quite often African immigrants, on-the-job training for certain positions is out of the question. In many cases, you know deep down in your heart that you can do the job much better and are probably more qualified than your White counterpart, but you would still be placed under that person and would most likely do most of the work while your colleague takes the glory.

The last hurray I had at Kodak was serving as their site manager and quality assurance/test manager for a software development center of excellence that I helped start in the Washington DC area in the late nineties to address the company's need to have a software development presence close to the nation's capital and the Northern Virginia high technology growth corridor. In that position, Kodak had the opportunity to let a well-qualified and experienced African immigrant run their software development center, but they failed to honor their own diversity pronouncements.

When the first development manager who was an African-American woman decided to move back to Rochester to be closer to her family, Kodak had a unique opportunity to tap an African immigrant or any other immigrant for that matter. But instead, the center was given to a manager based in Rochester who also happened to be a White man, while I acted in his place in Washington. He would visit the center once a month and was practically running the center remotely from Rochester while I handled the day-to-day activities of the center in Beltsville, Maryland.

The center's employee population was about 95 percent immigrants from all over the world—Africa, China, India, Korea, Russia, and Ukraine. Initially when the position opened up, all of a sudden there was an allegation against me by one American employee, albeit, an African-American who rumored that I had a placement agency that was providing contractors to the center. The Company's security department investigated the allegation for several months and found that there was no truth to the allegation and the Chief Technical Officer responsible for the center then closed the case without prejudice because it lacked merit. It was during this time that the new manager was chosen to oversee the center. I felt the allegation was designed to derail the possibility of an immigrant, albeit, an African immigrant from taking over full responsibility of the center. After that distraction, the center struggled for four more years under the new manager as it competed with the new manager's other development group in Rochester for funds and projects, and eventually was closed down in July of 2004 as a cost-cutting measure. These types of artificial barriers often make it impossible for certain members of our society to reach their full potential.

It's not uncommon to encounter West Africans who drive taxi cabs in major cities all over this country. When you engage them in a

conversation it's also not uncommon to find out
that majority of them have college degrees,
including masters and sometimes doctorate
degrees. As you probe further, their real
stories begin to unravel about how they have
simply given up because they couldn't stand the
discriminatory practices of the companies they
either worked for or applied to work for. So
they choose to go into a (potentially risky and
life-threatening) business in which they can
control their own destiny. While I do not
recommend giving up completely because one feels
discriminated against, it is obvious that there
is a large segment of the immigrant population
that could be making greater contributions to
the US economy, but cannot do so due to some
artificial barriers imposed by corporations. For
that reason, many West African immigrants fail
to reach their full potential in America.

Worthwhile Struggle

Before coming to America, I used to correspond with the World Bible Society (WBS). During that period I was assigned a WBS teacher. My teacher then lived in Ames, Iowa and her name was Mrs. Peter Garatoni. When I arrived in America, I contacted her to let her know that I was now in America to study. She wrote me a letter and I will never forget what she told me. She said, "In America, just like in any other country, there are good and bad. If you want to follow the bad, there is plenty to go around, and if you want to follow the good, there is also plenty to go around." The choice was mine. It is fair to say that I chose to follow the good things about America and I have never regretted it.

While my struggles, both in Nigeria before coming to America and after I arrived in

America, made life more difficult, there is no question that those struggles practically shaped my character and probably who I am today. I liken my struggles to Nussbaum's commandments for the American culture, especially the commandments that say, "No pain, No gain" and "God helps those who help themselves." These commandments translate to "get tough" and "do not whine, but work hard." These are all great principles that every successful person tends to live by. While I wished that I didn't have to go through those struggles to get to where I am today, I am consoled by the knowledge that amid all those hardships lay the triumphs that made the struggles worth going through. The struggles, to a large extent, shaped what I consider to be my triumphs and if you were to ask this immigrant to do it over again, I would probably not change much.

Chapter 3:   *The Triumphs*

"I have learned that SUCCESS is to be measured not so much by the
position that one has reached in life as by the OBSTACLES which one has
overcome while trying to succeed." - Bookcr T. Washington

Opening Doors

My father once told me, "You can become a
businessman overnight, but you cannot become a
bachelor's degree holder overnight." With that
guiding wisdom, I knew that the only way to even
stand a chance of making it in life was to stay
in school, graduate from secondary school, and
ultimately from a university. For me, success is
measured by not just how much I progress, but
also by how much people around me are
progressing.

My yardstick for measuring progress in any
family, community, or society is very simple,
and that is, how much is everybody contributing?
When everybody contributes, the burden is spread

across all involved, ensuring that no single person or a few individuals bear the brunt of the burden. This contrasts with the notion of one or a few people doing well while everybody else depends on them. Based on this principle, I can say for sure that I have indeed achieved a good deal of success since coming to America, despite the odds.

Human Capital Investment

I believe wholeheartedly in Nussbaum's commandment that states, "God helps those who help themselves". In my mind this implies that the people that you're trying to help are also willing and determined to help themselves. I recall one night in 1987, I had a dream and in my dream I was weeping to the point that when I woke up I was still crying. I had dreamt that I was confined in what looked like a concentration camp along with my younger siblings. I don't know exactly what had happened to my parents or my older siblings, but in the dream I had the responsibility of taking care of my younger siblings. For several weeks, I kept thinking of how to escape the concentration camp. One day, I managed to escape the camp by climbing down what seemed like a 14-foot fence with barbed wires. Before I escaped, I told my younger brother to look after the youngest ones until I came back for them. And I promised them that I would surely come back to get them. When I was leaving, my siblings and I cried and it was then that I woke up, but kept crying after I woke up. My wife noticed that I was crying and asked me what was wrong and I narrated the dream to her. It was after that dream that I resolved to help bring my siblings over to the United States.

That same year, my mother visited us and I reasoned then that her presence in the United

States could be the opportunity I needed to bring my siblings over. With my older brother already a United States citizen, I asked him to file a petition for a permanent resident status for our mother and he did. After my mother received her new permanent resident status, she then petitioned for her unmarried children and my father. While the cost of filing all those petitions was not pocket change and the responsibility fell on me because my brother was still in dental school at the time and could not help financially, I was willing to pay for them— no matter the cost. I made the sacrifice in part because I saw it as an investment and partly because of the dream I had. Three years later, they were all approved for immigrant visa. In 1991, my father and three of my siblings who were unmarried at the time immigrated to the United States.

When my younger siblings arrived, none of them had a college education. My younger brother had been an auto parts dealer in Nigeria, my youngest brother had just turned eighteen and recently graduated from high school, and my youngest sister was still in high school. After they arrived, my younger brother went back to college and completed a degree in automobile engineering and has been working for the city of Rochester ever since. He got married and has three wonderful children, two boys and a girl. His wife also completed a bachelor's degree in nursing and is now a registered nurse.

My youngest brother also entered college, but then had to respond to the call by the United States Selective Service and went on to serve as a US Marine. As his guardian at the time, one of the toughest and most gut-wrenching decisions I had to make was letting him join the

Marines. I felt that it was a good decision as it was another way for him to become a man. He went on to serve in the United States Marine Corps for 4 years of active duty and 6 years as a reservist. When he came out of active service, he became a US citizen, went back to school at the University of Maryland College Park and completed his undergraduate education. He then went on to Cooley Law School in East Lansing, Michigan where he graduated after two years with distinction. Today, he is a practicing attorney in the state of Maryland and the District of Columbia. My youngest sister continued her education and met her future husband at my own (second) wedding in 1994. Today, she is happily married with two sons and lives with her husband and children in Atlanta, Georgia.

The reason this is a triumph for me is because not only have they succeeded in life, but they became independent shortly after their arrival in America. If they were still in Nigeria, they would probably be dependent on me and my older brother today. So I feel triumphant because I fulfilled my dream's promise (literally) to go back and get my siblings out of a concentration camp, and it goes without saying that I have never been more grateful to the country that allowed me the opportunity to do so.

Landing a Corporate Job

Earlier I mentioned that I landed my first real corporate job four years after I had graduated from college. There is really more to the story than just applying for a job and then being offered a position by Kodak. Prior to what I call my first real corporate job, I had taken a job with another small company in Rochester, which came about as a result of working several

months for a temporary placement agency. Shortly
after accepting the job, I enrolled in a
graduate program at the State University of New
York, Brockport in 1985. With my background in
computer science, I enrolled in Brockport's
Master of Public Administration (MPA) program
with a concentration in Information Management
Systems. I pursued the degree program while
working full-time, and graduated in 1987.

SUNY Brockport: MPA degree
conferment, 1987

Rochester Institute of Technology: MS
degree conferment, 1989

Rochester Institute of Technology:
With my brother Dr. Kieran at the
graduation and my nephew Dana in the
background

Rochester Institute of Technology:
Receiving my MS degree in 1989

I must also mention that my company at the time paid for my tuition to pursue that graduate degree.

Meanwhile, in 1986, I enrolled in another graduate program in computer science at the Rochester Institute of Technology (RIT). This meant that at one point (for one full year), I was pursuing two masters' degrees from two different universities simultaneously and at the same time working full-time. This almost drove me crazy because I couldn't do anything else but work and go to school. After one year of this madness, I decided to stop my RIT computer science program in 1987 to concentrate on the MPA program. After completing the MPA program in the summer of 1987, I resumed my RIT graduate program.

When I resumed my computer science degree program in 1987, RIT had just introduced a new master's degree program in software development and management. I became interested in the curriculum and decided to switch. It was in that program that I met somebody (whom I would simply refer to by her first name, Nancy) who encouraged me to seek employment at Eastman Kodak Company. Nancy worked for Kodak at the time and was being sponsored by Kodak to complete the Software Development & Management program. There were only about seven of us that started the new graduate program, but by 1989 when RIT awarded its first master of science degree in software development and management, there were only three graduands (myself, Nancy, and another colleague named Wade), making three of us the pioneers of RIT's Software Development and Management program.

When I met Nancy and informed her of my interest in Kodak, she encouraged me to apply by providing me the name and contact address of the general manager of Kodak's Federal Systems division. Prior to that, one of my friends, Tobi, had secured a position in April of 1988 with Kodak's Clinical Diagnostics division as a Clinical Scientist, and had been pushing me to apply for a position at Kodak. Kodak would later disinvest in its Clinical Diagnostics products by selling that division to Johnson & Johnson. My friend Tobi kept telling me that with my background in computer science and a master's degree in information management systems, Kodak was the company for which I should be working. I kept telling him that I did not know anybody at Kodak and as such, wouldn't stand a chance whatsoever of landing a job with Kodak. That was what I thought, based on my perception of the company at the time. In its early years up until the late eighties, most people, me included, perceived Kodak as a nepotistic company (i.e., a company where people were hired because they had a family member or friend working for the company—father, son, daughter, wife, mother, grandfather, etc.). There was an unwritten understanding amongst locals that in order to secure employment at Kodak, you had to know somebody in the company. That was my understanding too, so when I was told to apply, I didn't think that I stood a chance since I had no family member who had ever worked for the company. My luck would change though, after I summoned the courage to apply, and especially after getting the name and address of the general manager of one of the company's largest divisions at the time.

In April of 1988, I decided to update my resume. I sent a letter to the then general manager of Kodak's Federal Systems with my resume attached. I did not hear anything from anybody for almost two months. One day in June, my phone at work rang and when I answered it, the person at the other end introduced himself as Jim Keady, the general supervisor of Kodak's Product Software Engineering division. He told me that he had received my resume from one of the general managers. He asked if I was still interested in pursuing a career at Eastman Kodak Company, and I answered affirmatively. He then said, "How would you like to attend an interview at Kodak next Wednesday?" I said, "Sure, I'd love to." And he said, "By the way, plan for spending the entire day with us, if you don't mind." I was flabbergasted because up until then, I had never been invited to or attended any interview that lasted more than one hour, and there I was being asked to plan for an all-day interview at a multi-national corporation that I had dreamt of working for.

I took a day off from my employer to attend the interview on the appointed date. The interview lasted from 9:00 AM until 3:00 PM, with one hour for lunch, for which they also paid. When I arrived, I was given an agenda that had been drawn prior to my arrival and the agenda showed that I would meet with eleven people, including the division's human resources representative at the end. By the time I left the company at 3:30 PM, the human resources representative had made me an offer for a position as software engineer with a salary that was more than double my salary at the time. I thanked the human resources representative and promised to study the offer, think about it, and then get back to him. Of course, I was bubbling with excitement inside, but remained calm until I got in my car.

When I returned home that afternoon, I called my older brother—who at the time was in dental school at SUNY Buffalo—with the good news. He asked whether or not I had accepted the offer. When I told him that I was yet to accept it, he said, "What are you waiting for?" Two days later, I called the human resources representative and accepted the offer. I also typed a formal acceptance letter and mailed it to him, confirming my acceptance of the offer. Later, when I called the Product Software Engineering Manager to thank him for the experience and the offer, he asked me for a date when I thought I could start work. I negotiated a date of August 15, 1988 as my starting date because I needed to tidy up and roundup a project that I was working on for my employer at the time.

On Friday August 12, 1988, members of the small company that I had been with for four years and had come to know individually hosted a farewell party for me at the office. It was like leaving another family behind, but I had to move on. On Monday August 15, 1988, I began a new career as a software engineer at Eastman Kodak Company that would last for sixteen years. It goes without saying that my life as I knew it in the small company that I worked for four years changed. There were good and bad experiences in the big corporate world, but overall, the experience I gained was something that I will always cherish as long as I live and my life was never the same again.

BONIFACE C. NWUGWO
Software Engineer
Product Software Engineering
Software Systems Division

EASTMAN KODAK COMPANY
100 Carlson Road
Rochester, New York 14653-9004

716 253-7862
KMX # 273-7862

My early days at Kodak

BONIFACE C NWUGWO
Lead Systems Test Engineer
Image Capture, IRS/DPS Program
Imaging Information Programs
Commercial & Govt Systems

EASTMAN KODAK COMPANY
6251 Ammendale Road
Beltsville, MD 20705

Office 301 470-5027
Fax 301 470-1068
KMX 716 231-9310

After relocating to Washington DC area

BONIFACE C. NWUGWO
QA & Test Manager
Washington Development Center
ESPC Systems Platform Center

EASTMAN KODAK COMPANY
11785 Beltsville Dr., Suite 1100
Beltsville, MD 20705-3119
email: bcn@kodak.com

Office 301 586-1739
KMX 235-1739
Fax 301 586-1770

After helping start a software development center of excellence in the Washington DC area

BONIFACE C. NWUGWO
Site Manager
Washington Development Center
CI-Output Systems Development

EASTMAN KODAK COMPANY
11785 Beltsville Drive, Suite 1100
Beltsville, MD 20705-3119
email: boniface.nwugwo@kodak.com

Voice 301 586-1739
KMX 235-1739
Fax 301 586-1770

My last 4 years at Kodak software development center of excellence in the Washington DC area

A moment in the office when my wife and the kids paid me a surprise visit at the Washington Development Center

With the Kodak CEO, Dan Carp and colleagues Daria and Alec Che Mponda at the opening of National Museum of African Arts, the Smithsonian, Washington DC

Receiving my doctorate degree from Capella's School of Business & Technology Chair.

Timeout to celebrate my birthday with my family and a couple of my Indian friends Raj Kosuri and Raju (not in picture) during my doctoral dissertation days.

Graduation Day from Capella with family members and my Committee Member & Dean of School of Technology, Dr. Kurt Linberg

Graduation Day from Capella with my wife Francisca carrying baby Denzel and my oldest, Brian in the background.

Graduation Day from Capella University in Minneapolis/St. Paul, MN with my family and some family friends.

L-R: My brother, Dr. Kieran, my mom and my dad at my graduation party

Achieving the American Dream

While the meaning of the American dream has evolved over the years from the original thinking of America's founders, today's American dream as widely understood by most Americans is still not that farfetched from the original principles. As defined by Gabor S. Boritt, the American Dream is the "faith held by many in the United States that through hard work, courage, and determination, rather than having been born in a particular social class, one can achieve a better life, usually in terms of financial prosperity."[8] Included in today's American dream is home ownership, being your own boss, having your own business, becoming rich and famous.

When my siblings immigrated to America in 1991, I sponsored and harbored them in my own home in Rochester, New York. I was able to provide them room and board because I had purchased my first home the year before. Using the knowledge I gained from studying various ways to make money in real estate, I was able to purchase my first home in Rochester. Within three years, my siblings had all moved on to become independent and I relocated to the Washington DC area on a job transfer by Kodak.

While I did not make any money from that first home transaction, I knew from that experience that home ownership is always a better option than renting. From that point on, I went on to acquire a new home and a few more rental properties in one of the most dynamic and progressive counties in Maryland, Howard County. After holding onto them for five to seven years, the prices on those homes doubled in value (and in some cases more than doubled), allowing me

---

[8] Gabor S. Boritt, *Lincoln and the Economics of the American Dream* (City: University of Illinois Press,

the opportunity to sell them and build my custom dream home from the ground up. While I am not a multi-millionaire, if net worth is measured by one's total assets minus total liabilities, and if a millionaire is a person whose net worth is equal to or greater than a million dollars, then I can proudly call myself a millionaire or very close to it. For a West African immigrant who came to America at the age of twenty with only $4,600 to his name, having a net worth close to a million dollars thirty years later, is not bad at all given all the odds that were against me.

While having a decent home, good cars and fairly good net worth are all good measures of one's success in life, for me, the greatest triumph is being married to one of the smartest, most intelligent, and beautiful women on earth and being blessed with four great children.

1994), 1.

After my first marriage ended, I met my soul mate, who has turned out to be the true wind beneath my wings. My wife is one of those tireless women who does not believe in sacrificing family or career at the expense of the other. She believes, as I do, that you can do both at the same time and that's exactly what both of us have been doing all these years.

We have four wonderful children, ages 17, 16, 15, and 12 at time of publication of this book and we had them while she was going to school. Shortly after we relocated to Maryland, she tried to pursue a master's degree in materials science engineering at the University of Maryland, College Park. While she was doing this, she had our first son and when our son was about three months old she became pregnant with our second child. After our second son was born, she came home one day and told me that she had been thinking about her career and the type of future she would like to have with the kids. She felt that with materials science engineering being a very specialized field, continuing a career in that area would amount to both of us being gone from the home 9 to 5. She wanted a career that would make it possible for at least one of us to be with the kids at all times when they are not in school.

For that reason, she contacted the University Of Maryland School Of Nursing in Baltimore and they informed her about their accelerated nursing program for people who already had a bachelor's degree. They told her all the prerequisites she would need. She then decided to pursue the accelerated program instead of materials engineering and spent two semesters completing the prerequisites. While completing the prerequisites, she applied for

admission and was admitted into the program
starting in the fall of 1998. At this time, she
was pregnant again with our third child and I
had also secured admission for a doctoral
program but I decided to quit mine to give her
all the support she needed to complete hers. By
December of 1999, she completed the accelerated
program, earning a bachelor's degree in nursing;
and by January of 2000, she sat for the
registered nurse board exam and passed it with
flying colors. By March 2000, she took up a job
at the University of Maryland Medical Center as
a registered nurse. Meanwhile, in December 1999,
I resumed my own doctoral program, completing it
in November of 2003 while working full time and
managing a software development center of
excellence for Kodak.

After my wife started working as a nurse,
she became pregnant one more time and gave birth

to our fourth child in April of 2001. Still not satisfied with just a bachelor's degree in nursing, she enrolled in a master's in nursing administration program at the University of Maryland, School of Nursing again. In December 2004, she completed her master's in nursing administration and was inducted into the Sigma Theta Tau International, the honor society of nursing. In 2006 she became a Senior Partner (or the equivalent of assistant nurse manager) and later a Senior Clinical Nurse II for the Transplant Unit.

It was not my intension to digress in telling the story of my wife. But the moral of the story is that with determination, one can actually have a career and family at the same time and still be successful in both areas. While it may not be the best way to go, for a lot of West Africans in America, it is the only

way. And, as far as I'm concerned, my greatest
triumph is having a beautiful, smart, and
wonderful wife who is not afraid to pursue a
decent career with a family to show for it.

A Milestone at a Time

One of the good things about aging is that
you get wiser as time passes and you get to
assess and re-assess the past in order to plan
for your future. I now see life as a series of
milestones that must be met one milestone at a
time. Since I came to America, I can honestly
say that I have accomplished all the goals I set
for myself and some more. I completed a
bachelor's degree, becoming the second person in
my family after my older brother to earn a
college degree. Since then I have completed two
masters' degrees and one doctorate degree,
becoming the first in my family to earn a PhD.

I have also completed a successful career spanning over twenty five years in both small and large corporations. I have now embarked on a new milestone to build a new career of managing my own business in order to be in control of my own destiny for the rest of my years instead of depending on others for employment. I have already started an IT consulting business, using my vast skills and training in information technology to provide IT services to businesses and government agencies. I have embarked on a new project to establish a computer manufacturing company in Nigeria that specializes in the assembling and marketing of standards-based, made-to-order computer systems, software, computer accessories and computer services directly to consumers in Nigeria and other West African countries. This firm will provide custom-built desktop computers, laptops, and computer accessories to meet individual needs as well as the needs of businesses, educational institutions, and healthcare and governmental organizations.

My next milestone is to nurture a Foundation that my wife and I established to focus on reducing water-borne diseases by promoting safe water supply, and to expand educational opportunities in Nigeria and in America that serves to enhance and promote awareness of the extremely poor water supply conditions and lack of educational opportunities in Nigeria.

The Foundation helps to improve community access to clean water and sanitation by constructing new wells, and training of local people to manage and maintain the water supply. The Foundation sponsors borehole water drilling projects to provide access to clean water for low-income and village dwellers.

The Foundation also funds scholarships to expand access to university education for low-income students with interests in engineering, computer science and agricultural engineering. Every year, thousands of academically-gifted students are unable to pursue university degrees because their families cannot afford the rising costs of higher education. Very few low-income students can expect to graduate from a university in Nigeria. This is not due to a lack of talent but rather due to the high costs of tuition, and the fact that many students graduate from secondary school without the skills they need to succeed in the university.

The way I see it, my job is to continue knocking on doors to open them for new opportunities for myself and others and take advantage of those opportunities that arise as long as God gives me breath.

Supernatural Interventions

As I look back to my life pre- and post-emigration from Nigeria, I can't help but be thankful to the Almighty God when I count my blessings. Obviously, every single triumph that has come my way could not have been possible without the intervention of the Lord. I remember one day in November of 1986 that my life could have ended, but for some supernatural reason, it did not. I was travelling to New York City from Rochester one Friday evening. On the way, it started snowing. I thought the snow would stop just as it started, but little did I know that upstate New York was just getting its first major lake-effect snow of the year. Many people, including myself, were caught unawares and had not changed their radial tires in preparation for the winter season. I tried to follow the tracks made by a truck that had passed a few minutes ahead of me. What I didn't know was that the truck had exposed the ice that had formed underneath the snow.

After about a mile of following the tracks left by the truck, I realized that I was making 55 miles per hour, which was a little too fast for the condition on the ground. So I tried to slow down and tapped my brakes. But as soon as I hit my brakes, the car started skidding and spun around 360 degrees, three times. It happened so fast that within a twinkle of an eye, it was all over and my car came to a stop about three feet from a gully that had no guard rails. The nearest vehicle at the time was about a mile away, so I cranked my ignition again and the car started and I drove off. When I finally got to New York City about eight hours later and recounted my ordeal to my friend, I became scared. As I told my story, it occurred to me that I could have ended in the gully and probably nobody would have found me because it was getting dark.

Another supernatural moment was when my wife was spared from serious injuries or even death from two car accidents within a space of two weeks. The first one was on Friday, December 2, 2005. About two months prior, I had leased a new car for my business. But on that day, I drove my old car to my client's location in Annandale, Virginia. About 1:25 P.M., my cell phone rang and the number that appeared was unfamiliar. When I answered the phone, I was surprised to hear my wife's voice. She said that she was calling from the Howard County General Hospital's Emergency Department and that she was involved in an accident, but I should not bother coming back immediately because she was alright and would be going home shortly. What she didn't tell me was how serious and dangerously close to being fatal the accident was.

My wife had just picked up the youngest of our four children from the kindergarten at 11:00 A.M. and decided to get some gasoline because the car was almost empty. She drove to an Exxon station about two miles from our home. After filling up the tank, she proceeded to head home. While trying to exit the gas station and make a left turn onto the busy Route 103, the motorist from her left side slowed down and motioned at her to come out because the traffic light had just turned red. As she proceeded to join the road, a dump truck that was behind the motorist jumped the line and hit the driver's side of the front of the car, missing her by few inches.

Although she hit her head against the driver's side window and her face on the deployed safety bag, other than some headaches and a couple of weeks of physical therapy for whiplash, she did not sustain any major injury. My son, who was strapped in his car seat in the back, did not sustain any major injuries either, other than minor cuts from the shattered glasses that sprayed him. A couple of days later, when I visited the facility to where the car was towed and saw how much damage was done to the vehicle, it dawned on me how close to death my wife came. I realized then that it was definitely a supernatural intervention that prevented me from becoming a widower prematurely.

Two weeks later on December 25, 2005, she went back to work for the first time after the accident. The whole family was gathered in our home as we hosted the Christmas party and I tried to talk her out of going to work that night. But she explained that she had to go because she was already scheduled to work that Christmas night. But on her way to work, just five minutes after she left home, she called me and said that she had been involved in an accident. I couldn't believe what I was hearing and didn't know how to break the news to the family, so I whispered the news to one of my brothers-in-law. He and I drove to the scene of the accident and luckily, she was not seriously injured. What had happened was that, while she was trying to join I-95 North, another motorist who was behind her tried to speed up and join the highway before her. The young man had miscalculated and rammed her from the rear, totaling the vehicle. Again, other than the whiplash she suffered, she did not sustain any major injury. Obviously, without some supernatural interventions from above, none of my or my wife's triumphs would have been possible.

Presenting our first born for baptism

Our first son's baptism

On my wife's MS graduation. From L-R: Brian, my wife, self, Denzel, Allen and Jaine

At my own graduation. L-R: Allen, self, Denzel, Brian, my wife & Jaine

Visiting home in Nigeria in December of 2011. L-R: Boniface, Denzel, Allen, Jaine, Francisca and Brian

PART II: COURAGE, STRUGGLES AND TRIUMPHS OF OTHER WEST AFRICAN IMMIGRANTS

"Rejoice in your hope, be patient in tribulation, be
constant in prayer."
(Romans 12:12 (RSV))

Chapter 4:   *Determined to Make a Difference*

Fred Kema never thought of going to America until circumstance compelled him to. Kema and a few of his classmates had been barred by their Rector from taking the West African School Certificate examination when they were due to take it. In short, Kema and his schoolmates were delayed one year from passing out of secondary school simply because they had sat for the General Certificate of Education O/Level (an external exam) the year before. Their punishment for taking an external exam was suspension from school for one year.

Kema was a junior seminarian and the Catholic seminary schools were too strict to the point that mere sitting for an external examination without the express permission of the Rector could lead to a student's suspension or outright expulsion. Although Kema and his friends were not expelled from school, they were suspended for one full year, so instead of graduating from secondary school in 1978 as he was supposed to, Kema finished in 1979. That suspension and one-year delay caused him so much grief that it became the beginning of the end of his seminary ambitions just as it was for most of his colleagues who received the same punishment.

Having lost one year to suspension, most of Kema's friends and mates that he started out with had moved on to senior seminary, others had found jobs, and some had gained admission into universities. A few had chosen to travel abroad to the United Kingdom or the United States to pursue their university education.

Increasingly disinterested in continuing with seminary school, Kema began thinking of leaving the country for the United States too. So immediately after graduating from junior seminary in 1979 at the age of 18 (seminary school students also sat for the West African School Certificate exam in order to graduate), he began planning for his departure, but first he had to get his mother's consent.

Convincing Mother to Let Go

Kema was an only child of his mother with several half brothers and sisters. Kema had never been away from his mother before (at least longer than a couple of weeks), let alone to talk of traveling to a foreign country for years. He was so attached to his mother and his mother was so emotionally attached to him that he did not know how to leave his mother for a foreign country without breaking her heart. So, when he first thought about the possibility of leaving for the United States, his greatest obstacle was convincing his mother that he could live independently in America and that his mother could live without him.

Kema's mother had been a midwife for a long time so she knew the value of education. So while Kema was worried about how to convince his mother about his plan to go abroad to study, his mother was already making plans for him to go abroad to the United States to continue his education. She had already had some discussions with her nephews, who were already well-educated and knew the value of a quality college education. While apprehensive about letting their auntie's only child go to the United States, they all agreed that sending Kema to America would probably do him more good than harm. So as it turned out, Kema did not have too much convincing to do after all. The only thing he had to do was to muster some courage to inform his mother about his own plans. And when he did, he was very surprised as to how both of their plans converged. As it turned out, the main obstacle for Kema was not convincing his mother to let him go, but raising the money for the trip as well as how he would sustain himself when he got to America.

Raising the Money

For many West African students with the hope of traveling to the United States to study, raising the money to make the costly journey is a major obstacle. Kema was no stranger to the problem of lack of funds, but was determined as a young man to make the insurmountable possible. For his own contribution, Kema secured a teaching job in one of the local commercial schools in the village to help with minor expenses for his trip, while he went through the admission and student advisory processes. A commercial school is a vocational institution that specializes in typing and secretarial studies. While his income from the teaching job was enough for pocket money, the main financial aspect of his plan still needed to be addressed.

Kema's kindred had a student scholarship program for people entering into universities. Although they called it a scholarship, it was more like a loan as the money had to be repaid after the recipient graduated from the university. The "loan/scholarship" program as it was called was geared more toward students studying in their local universities, rather than those going abroad to study because of the amount involved.

The amount awarded to students was about the equivalent of $6,000 for the entire four-year undergraduate degree program. That amount was barely enough for one year's tuition and board in a State University in New York for a foreign student paying out-of-state fees. However, Kema applied and was awarded the loan/scholarship. With that amount and his mother's own savings, he was able to raise about $7,000, enough for one full year of tuition and board, and also enough to be issued a student visa by the United States Embassy. Having secured his F-1 student visa to study in the United States, Kema looked forward to his journey to America; but like other West Africans who made similar journeys before him, he underestimated the challenges that would face him once he got there.

Homesickness

One of the reasons that Kema made up his mind to go to the US to continue his studies was largely because two of his cousins were already studying in the school that he was going to attend. Despite having some cousins already in America, he still knew that it would not be easy staying without his mother. He started being homesick even before he left home. To alleviate his homesickness, he brought with him some mementos of his home and mother to ease the pain, including some pictures of his mother and some family group pictures.

There were no telephones at home so he couldn't call his mother as he would have liked to; instead he depended on handwritten mails, which were time consuming because they tended to be lengthy. It was not uncommon for Kema to spend two-to-three days composing a letter to his mother and likewise, reading his mother's replies often took a couple of days as they were always double-digit pages long.

However, after a couple of semesters, his school workload began to occupy his time more and more such that he was no longer getting enough time to do his school assignments, work, and other collegiate activities, not to mention writing several pages of letters to his mother as he used to. The monthly letters became bimonthly, and pretty soon quarterly and eventually every six months. His mother's letters became less frequent too, a sign that both of them had gotten used to the separation.

Harsh Realities

Most immigrants that come to America, particularly West Africans, often face harsh conditions from day one, especially those who arrive during the winter season. Take for example, Kema, who arrived in New York for the first time on January 14, 1981 on a bitter cold day. The temperature at JFK Airport that day was probably well below zero degrees Fahrenheit, with considerable snow on the ground. Coming from Africa, he did not quite understand how cold it could get during the winter seasons. So he was wearing his three-piece summer suit when he arrived in New York on that bitter cold morning of January 14, 1981 only to be greeted with the harsh realities of the winter season.

When Kema first stepped out of the JFK airport, he was in the company of another new arrival that he had met on the plane. The first thing Kema noticed was that the ground was covered with some white stuff. That was his first time seeing snow. The next observation

Kema and his friend made was that almost everybody they saw was smoking cigarette. They both thought that smoking was how people overcame the cold weather, so his friend decided to buy himself a pack of cigarettes. He lit up a cigarette for the first time in his life, but despite his new-found habit of smoking, he was still cold since smoking cigarette was not the cure.

Getting Duped

All Kema wanted to do when he arrived at JFK International Airport in New York was to get to LaGuardia Airport and catch a flight to Rochester, New York. Because of the bitter cold, when a taxi driver approached him to take him to LaGuardia, Kema did not hesitate to follow him to his cab, which was running and heated inside. The cab driver promised to get him a winter coat as well as take him to LaGuardia. However, the taxi driver asked him to pay $300 for the taxi fare and the winter coat. The cab driver purchased a winter coat for Kema worth about $75.00 and charged him $225 (average cab fare then was about $25) for the taxi fare from JFK to LaGuardia Airport.

Kema did not know that he had been duped until he arrived in Rochester and narrated his experience to his cousins. His cousins told him not to despair since the cab driver was at least kind enough to purchase a winter coat for him, took him to the airport and also kept him warm. But the truth is that many Africans and other immigrants that come to America the first time are often taken advantage of by taxi drivers that take them from one airport to another. In most cases, they end up paying ten to twenty times what it normally costs for a taxi fare.

Kema was not the first nor would he be the last. When he learned that others got it even worse than he did—for example, another West African paid $1,200 for a taxicab from JFK to LaGuardia— he stopped grieving. There were many more realities about America than just being taken advantage of by cab drivers.

For somebody like Festus Wale, who came here in the mid-seventies, not only was he taken advantage of by a cab driver, but he was practically robbed of his only means of sustenance when he arrived. Unlike some of his counterparts who at least knew somebody in America to guide them, Wale did not know a single soul in America when he arrived in 1974. With only $400 (in money order) in his pocket, he set out for the United States. He had already remitted his school fees directly to his school before coming. The money he had was supposed to pay for his books, room and board, transportation, personal effects and food. When he arrived at JFK, a taxi driver took $125 out of his $400 just to take him to LaGuardia Airport.

Preparing to Lead

Kema knew that he could not fail because that would mean disappointing a lot of people, especially his mother. As the oldest of his father's children and the first in his family to go to college, there were a lot of people counting on him. Although the pressure for Kema was unbearable; for many West Africans, such pressure is normal. One of the challenges for Kema was how to accomplish the

enormous task of graduating from college
in a short period so as to begin helping
his father with the daunting task of
putting more than ten of his half
brothers and sisters through school.

Graduating from Alternate College

SUNY Brockport had a program called the
Alternate College, which has since been renamed
the Delta College. The Alternate College program
was an alternative to the traditional College of
Brockport's General Education program. The
Alternate College offered an interdisciplinary
approach to the required undergraduate liberal
arts and science courses of the traditional
college. All majors and certification programs
offered at the College were compatible with the
Alternate College program. Due to the way the
Alternate College courses were structured (most

were four-hour credit courses), it was possible

for Alternate College students to graduate in

three years instead of the normal four years

because the total credits required for

graduation were ninety-six as opposed to one

hundred and twenty required by the traditional

General Education program.

Due to the high cost of tuition for foreign

students, many African students, including Kema,

saw the Alternate College as a way to obtain

their undergraduate education in three years;

saving themselves one full year of tuition and

fees. Although the Alternate College required

only 96 credits for graduation, Kema completed

120 credits for graduation and was still able to

graduate in three years. He then completed a

Master of Public Administration degree in one

year. So in four years, Kema was able to earn a

baccalaureate in psychology and a master's degree in public administration. By his fifth year in this country, he had started a PhD program at SUNY Buffalo and would later take a break to concentrate on family matters. After almost a ten-year hiatus, he continued the doctoral program and eventually earned a PhD in educational administration.

Landing Jobs

Kema became involved with a girl while he was completing his undergraduate program and they eventually got married just before his graduation. By the time he completed his master's degree program, pressure from home was mounting. More responsibilities were being created for Kema, albeit by his father, who continued to have children unabated, despite his retirement and limited income. For that reason,

Kema had to quit the doctoral program in order to help out his father.

He secured a night job as a counselor to young men and women with psychological and developmental challenges. In addition, he worked a day job as a legislative analyst to the mayor. After he completed his PhD, he accepted another position as principal management analyst for the city's school district and later, the director of human resources of a major public school system.

Chapter 5:   Against All Odds

Stranger by Fate

For many West African immigrants to America, their fates are often determined by events out of their control. Such events include civil wars, sectarian or tribal conflicts, and political victimization. Liberians were no strangers to such conflicts in the eighties and nineties. Nelson Wey was one of those immigrants for whom circumstances beyond his control brought him to America.

In a way, Wey was one of the lucky ones because he left his country just before political and tribal conflicts erupted in the early eighties. He had traveled to Europe to study medicine. Shortly after he arrived in England, on April 12, 1980, a group of non-commissioned soldiers led by Sergeant Samuel Doe assassinated the leader of his country, President William Richard Tolbert. Sergeant Doe became the Military Head of State of Liberia following the assassination of President Tolbert, an act that eventually plunged the country into a civil war that would last for almost two decades. By 1989, Liberia had descended into a full-blown civil war.

After graduating from medical school and completing his internship, Wey thought about returning home, but then realized that he had no country to return to since Liberia had plunged into anarchy. With no stable or safe country to return to, Wey decided to go to the US for more advanced training and hopefully, to practice medicine in America. Given

what he had read and heard about America—
how it was the best place for high quality,
advanced training, especially in the medical
field—Wey felt that giving up his residency
spot in the United Kingdom for a chance
to study in the United States would be a
better option for him. Little did he know
that the rosy picture of America that he had
would be influenced by race and the color of his
skin. He would also face other barriers that he
did not anticipate.

Certification Red Tape

For many years, international medical
graduates (IMGs) have always made up about one-
fourth of the physician population in the United
States, a trend which has continued until today.
While Wey knew that all international medical
graduates who wish to enter an accredited

residency or fellowship program in the US must be certified by the Educational Commission for Foreign Medical Graduates (ECFMG) before they can enter the program, he was not prepared for the bureaucratic barriers with which he would be confronted. Wey knew that to be granted an unrestricted license to practice in the US, he must first pass a three-step exam, known as the United States Medical Licensing Examination (USMLE), for certification designed for IMGs.

In addition to these requirements, he must also complete a three- to seven-year post-graduate medical program (residency) accredited by the Accreditation Council for Graduate Medical Education (ACGME), which is a requirement for anybody who wants to practice medicine in the United States. What he did not know, however, was the amount of money and bureaucratic red tape that he would have to go through in order to qualify to practice. He successfully passed both the Step 1 and Step 2 exams of the United States Medical Licensure Examination as well as the Clinical Skills Assessment (CSA) by the Educational Commission for Foreign Medical Graduates, but could not match into the Post Graduate Year 1 (PGY-1) or residency positions. It took a couple of years for him to secure a PGY-1 position.

Finding a Match

As he came to find out later, one of the reasons that Wey did not match into a PGY-1 position is that he lacked American letters of recommendation from crucial domestic clinical work in the United States. Not only was he

lacking letters of recommendation, the odds were

stacked up against him. For example, while slow

but continuous improvements have been made in

the number of international medical graduates

accepted into residency programs since the

1980s, nonetheless, less than 60 percent of IMGs

are matched every year. According to the

Association of American Medical Colleges (AAMC),

in the 2003 Match for residency programs, of the

5,029 international medical graduates who were

active participants in the 2003 Match, 2,799 or

55.7% were matched to PGY-1 positions.[9]

So for the first two years, Wey

received the usual response from

residency directors, "We regret to inform you

that for fear of patient safety and potential

---

[9] AAMC, April 2003 Reporter "Record Number of Residency Positions Filled in 2003 Match."

lawsuits, we are unable to interview you or offer you a spot in our residency program." But according to Wey, the process was inherently prejudiced. He could not land any clinical work that would provide him the necessary hands-on experience and consequently some letters of recommendation. American-trained medical students could get these letters of recommendations when they took their electives in US hospitals, but since Wey did not attend medical school in the United States, he was out of luck.

However, Wey was so determined not to fail that he decided to complete an observership program (i.e., a program for physicians from outside the US who want to experience American medical practice as an observer for a few weeks without actually participating in the delivery of care) at a hospital. The observership program proved to be a total waste of effort and money because it did not offer him the necessary hands-on experience that residency directors were looking for.

Finally, he enrolled in a six-month externship program for US clinical experience designed for international medical graduate physicians who seek placement in post graduate US medical training. At the completion of the externship program, the physician with whom he was working wrote a letter of recommendation for him reflecting his clinical competence and professionalism.

Armed with the letter of recommendation and his Medical Licensing Examination certifications, he was able to match a PGY-1 position (residency), even though he had to look in the inner city hospitals where many American graduates do not want to work because of the related urban problems. After being matched with the Thomas Jefferson University Hospital, an inner city hospital in Philadelphia, Wey proceeded to secure a medical license to practice for the state of Pennsylvania.

Wey's challenges as an intern were compounded as an international medical graduate (IMG). These included such things as learning to conduct patient interviews. As Wey would come to discover, communication with patients and other residents were impaired due to language and accent problems. He wished that he had taken language, slang, and accent reduction training. A course in American culture would have been helpful, Wey concluded.

Integrating into Work Role

When Nelson Wey arrived in America, he thought that his problems had been solved, but

actually, his struggles were just beginning.
Armed with his medical degree, his
certifications, letters of recommendation, and
his first placement in a residency program, Wey
felt that he was now ready to do what he came to
do in America, which was to practice medicine.
Having invested so much time and energy in being
matched for a PGY-1 residency position, he felt
that he was ready to "kick the tires," so to
speak.

However, he quickly realized that the
dynamics of the hospital organization he joined
were far different from what he was used to.
Although he viewed himself as knowledgeable and
experiential as well as someone who was not
resistant to change, he felt lost in following
the new rules of the game. Terminologies like
"evidence-based medicine," "managed care,"
"insurance and contracting," "physician practice

management," and "physician-staff relationship" were common, yet he was not sure of how they related to his future success as a physician. At the same time, he was not sure how to ask his director and wondered whether it was something he should even bring up with the resident director, which made him more frustrated.

Financial Difficulties

Almost every medical student faces some financial difficulties (unless the student's parents are filthy rich), but Wey's financial difficulties were exacerbated by the civil strife that tore up his country while he was away. While many international students who have full and sustained sponsorship from private or public sources can sail through their education without worrying about finances, a majority of them often face financial problems at some point during the course of their studies. Initially, many students have adequate financial support when they arrive to begin their studies, but then something happens to change their situation.

Wey's circumstances changed when his country plunged into civil strife. He had a scholarship to study in the United Kingdom, but the coup and subsequent civil strife in his country caused the cancellation of the scholarship. Funding from his own private sources (mainly his parents) were not adequate partly because they could not provide the full amount, and partly because the government had restricted the remitting of any amount of money abroad. His inability to receive funds from his home country due to the political instability proved to be a major impediment in attaining registration while in medical school. If it weren't for the fact that his school gave him some financial aid, he could have become destitute and eventually wouldn't have made it through medical school.

When he reached America, financing was again an impediment to his career pathway. The certifications, exams, interim courses to obtain practical clinical experiences, and letters of recommendation required a lot of money that Wey did not have. Fortunately though, he met some people from his country when he arrived in America. One of them helped him to secure alternative financing by co-signing with him to obtain a student loan. With that, he was able to manage until he secured a residency position.

At the Brink of Quitting

Wey had heard about the hectic hours resident doctors must endure for the duration of their residency program, but he did not quite understand it until after his first full week.

For his first week, he worked a little over 100 hours being awake and treating patients around the clock. Incidentally, that would be the best week for Wey as a resident because as time went on, Wey's typical schedule became 30-hour shifts, six days a week, with little or no sleep. As Wey put it, "long hours put my stamina to the test and I thought that I was going crazy."

For his first year of residency, Wey's typical day started at 7:00 A.M. and ended at 1:00 P.M. the following day. Wey usually arrived at the hospital at 7:00 A.M. By 7:30 A.M., all the residents working that day attended a lecture on topics ranging from congestive heart failure to renal failure treatment. The lecture often ended at 8:15 A.M. after which Wey would start conducting rounds.

Attending rounds lasted from 8:15 A.M. to 10:30 A.M. daily. All of the patients cared for by the interns were examined. Wey and other interns would discuss their new patients and any problems with the resident, and plan the day's work. When work rounds ended, interns initiated the day's plan.

From noon until 5 P.M., the interns remained available to handle whatever came up. Sometimes, Wey checked on patients or helped out in the emergency room. Other times, he ended up answering phone calls. The afternoon was occupied admitting new patients, performing procedures, and doing the work of caring for patients. Interns admit on-call every fourth night, and on a normal admitting day an intern admits up to five new patients.

After ten hours at work, all but two of the residents would punch out. The two remaining residents would begin the night shift or what

they called the "moonlight shift." When

"moonlighting," Wey would continue to check on

patients and handle other chores, including

answering the phone, from 5 P.M. until 7 A.M.

Some nights, if everything was quiet (and they

rarely were), he would sneak off to catch a nap,

with his pager serving as a backup alarm clock.

If Wey got two to four hours of sleep without

the pager going off, he felt better the next

morning.

When the moonlighters began their twenty-

fourth hour, the residents who went home for a

good night's sleep would return to work, and it

would be time again for the moonlighters to

attend their second 7:30 a.m. meeting of the

shift. Wey and his fellow moonlighters were not

allowed to take on new patients after the

meeting, but were required to continue to check

on the patients they had been caring for since the previous morning. The shift would finally end at 1 p.m. and Wey would get to go home for a good night's sleep.

The insanely long hours at work brought Wey to the brink of quitting. However, whenever he remembered all the hardships he had endured throughout his life, he would become inspired again to keep going by telling himself that he was at the last mile of his marathon and that very soon it would be over. Wey did hang on to complete the program.

Making Lemonade Out of Lemons

When Nelson Wey completed his residency, he sat down to reflect one day, and he asked himself one question, "How did I do it?" Of course, he could not come up with a straight answer, but deep down he knew that it was just hard work and determination to succeed that made it possible. Wey's success story is not different from many immigrants—and West African immigrants in particular—who come to America with little or nothing, but often take on menial jobs to support themselves while obtaining their education. Like others, Wey simply used his ingenuity and work ethic to advance himself professionally and financially.

Those same opportunities are available to those born here, of course, but sometimes we take them for granted. Those who come from other nations and cultures do not take such opportunities for granted. They know that our free enterprise system and acceptance of people for their abilities, rather than status, give all an opportunity to succeed.

Chapter 6:   Determined to Survive

For many West Africans, venturing to America and eventually staying is just a matter of survival, especially for the women. In most cases, many of the women that come to America are lured into making the journey with the goal of joining their husbands and fiancés only to be abandoned by the same men that brought them here. Many arrive on a fiancé visa, which mandates that they get wedded to their fiancés within ninety days of their arrival in America. Some of these women have made the trip only to discover that their husbands or fiancés had lied to them.

Pretty soon, they begin to find out how incompatible they are or if they are already married, how far apart they have grown. Some discover that their husbands or fiancés have been cheating on them for so long that they almost immediately start having problems upon their arrival in America, which eventually leads to separation and divorce. This explains why divorce rate among Africans in America is higher than the divorce rate of Africans in Africa. Maria Manseh was one of those West African women that came to America with the intention of reconnecting with her husband and raising their two daughters together, only to be abandoned by her husband barely two months after her arrival.

Manseh was an accomplished primary (elementary) school teacher in her native Ghana before she immigrated to the United States. She was, in fact, the headmistress of her school the last three years of her teaching career before her husband told her to start getting ready to join him in America. She and her husband had one daughter before her husband left home. Five years later, she became pregnant again when her husband visited them from America and gave birth to another baby girl. She took care of their two girls while he was studying in America. When she was told by her husband that he was working on bringing her and the kids over to America to join him, she felt that she needed to acquire some other skills that could enable her obtain a job in America, and help her husband in providing the best opportunities for their daughters. She had heard about the shortage of nurses in America, so she decided to get training in nursing.

Career Change

For the last three years before Manseh came to America, she went to a vocational nursing school. She did this while still the headmistress of an elementary school. Every day after school, she attended classes for a nursing program. Not too long after she began the training, a rumor spread around the school that Mrs. Manseh was studying to become a nurse. The students thought that it was funny and nicknamed her "Madam Nurse Headmistress." Although she did not think that it was funny, she did not allow the rumors to bother her, remaining undeterred from pursuing her new career. She successfully completed the training after three years.

She had just completed the nursing program when their visas were approved at the beginning of summer in 2004. With her and her children's visas approved, there was nothing else she could do but to resign her teaching position as the headmistress and to say goodbye to her pupils and colleagues.

Sacrificing Career for Family

Giving up her career as a teacher and leaving her students behind for an unknown world was a gut-wrenching decision for Manseh, but she had to do it for the sake of re-uniting her family. She did not know what to expect in America. Would she be able to adjust to the new world? Would the new world welcome her and her children? These were all questions she was dealing with within herself.

After deliberating over these questions for some time and consulting with her mother and siblings, she made the ultimate decision to leave everything behind, quit the only career she had ever known, uproot her children, and join her husband in America.

Obtaining a Visa

Manseh never had any ambitions of immigrating to the US, despite her husband's insistence. Her husband had made an attempt before to obtain visas for her and the girls, but they were turned down at their first attempt. After that experience, she resolved within herself to stay home with her children and made peace with the possibility of not joining her husband in America. She settled on the idea that her husband could visit her and the kids at least once a year, perhaps during the Christmas seasons. So, she was no longer enthusiastic about obtaining a visa to travel to the United States despite the incessant pressure from her friends and mother.

In January of 2004, her husband informed her that he had filed another petition for a visa on her and the kids' behalf. She did not take the news seriously because she felt that it would be like the first time. However, six months later she received a letter of invitation from the American Embassy for an interview. To travel from her town to the American Embassy is usually a one-day trip. She really did not want to subject her girls to the same ordeal they went through four years earlier. She called her husband and told him that she was skeptical about going. Her husband convinced her to give it another chance. He had sent her all the supporting documents that she would need for the interview, so she changed her mind and decided to attend the interview.

On the day before the interview, she and her two girls boarded a bus for an overnight ride to Accra, arriving very early in the morning the next day. They freshened up at the bus station and caught a taxi straight to the American Embassy. To her greatest surprise, they were asked to come back in a couple of days for their visas. She phoned her husband from there and gave him the good news. The husband did not sound very excited about the good news on the phone, but she did not take it to mean anything. She and her girls checked into a motel, rather than travel back to their village to come back again in two days. When they went back to the Embassy on the third day, their passports had been stamped with visas. They caught a taxi to the bus station for an overnight bus ride back to their village to start preparing for their departure.

Getting Flight Tickets

For Manseh and the two girls to travel to the United States, they would need at least a one-way flight ticket to Baltimore or Washington

D.C. The husband was supposed to purchase the tickets and confirm it before they could depart. They waited for two weeks, they did not hear from him. One month passed, there was still no ticket. He called and told them that he was getting certain things ready for their arrival and would be getting back to them very soon.

After three months, Manseh began to wonder whether her husband really wanted them to join him in America. Perhaps he was hoping that they would not be issued visas, but when they were actually issued visas, he started back-peddling. Eventually, in July of 2004, four months after they secured their visas, the husband sent their flight tickets. One week later, Manseh said her final goodbyes to her students, staff, teachers, mother, and siblings; and headed to America with her two daughters (aged 6 and 11), and her credentials—including her newly acquired nursing certificate and transcripts.

Facing Abandonment

There is no worse feeling than the feeling of abandonment in a strange land. For many West African immigrants, especially the women that come to America to join their husbands or fiancés, it is a reality that occurs more often that a lot of people are not aware of. The abandonment often happens during the early days when the women arrive in America, the period in their lives that they are most vulnerable because they do not know the system yet and in most cases, do not have a support system that they can rely on. That was the case of Maria Manseh, who prior to her trip to America, had a premonition that her husband may not have wanted her and the kids to join him in America. When she arrived and was abandoned two months later, she felt that she should have trusted her gut feeling and stayed home.

Wrong Orientation

When Manseh and her two daughters arrived in America, they were relieved to have survived the long journey and finally reunited with her husband. The kids were excited to be reunited with their father and to be a family again; however, the excitement quickly fizzled out after a couple of days of staying with him. They arrived in America sometime in July, which was the middle of the summer season when the weather was very good and there were potentially a lot of things and places to see, so they thought.

When you are new in a place, the best way to get acclimated to the new environment is to go out and explore the area. Their first week was spent indoors, so they thought perhaps it was a way of letting them recuperate from their jet lag. By the second week, other kids around their neighborhood were knocking on their doors for the kids to come out and play, but the two girls would not venture outside to play, and neither would their mother, Manseh. Other neighbors came around to say hello and offer their assistance for anything she and her daughters might need, but she declined every gesture that her neighbors made.

As her neighbors would learn later, it was not that Manseh and her kids did not want to come out; rather, her husband had warned them that talking to any of their neighbors or going outside the house without him carried a hefty consequence. He was instead giving them the wrong orientation about America so that he could control them as he wished. This cost her and the kids some valuable lessons they could have learned such as how to go about registering the children for school, where to go shopping for food and clothes, and so on. Ordinarily, the husband was supposed to tell her and/or show her how to do these things, but he did not. The new school season was fast approaching, just about four weeks away and she did not know what to do.

New School System

Because Manseh was a trained teacher and a former headmistress of an elementary school, not knowing what to do with respect to her children's education was very unsettling for her. She did not know the new school system and was eager to find out, but her husband kept promising to take her and the kids to the school for registration. She eventually found out about the school calendar from one of her neighbors, who also had elementary school-aged kids. When she did, she realized that the new school year was only three weeks away. About two weeks before schools re-opened, her husband finally took her and their two girls to their neighborhood elementary school for placement.

The new school system was foreign to Manseh. The biggest difference for her was the amount of paperwork and proof parents were required to present in order to register children for school. They had to produce information such as a signed original house lease or deed, current utility bill with their name and address, each child's proof of birth as well as proof of immunization, and other requirements. Since primary and secondary education is publicly funded in America as compared to her native country, Manseh would come to understand later why all that information was needed.

The husband could not provide all the required documents the same day, so they had to go home and gather all the necessary documents to come back another day. When they finally returned with all the required paperwork, the girls were given a placement test and placed in second and sixth grades according to their ages.

Surviving first winter

When schools re-opened after Labor Day, the summer was over and the chilly days of autumn in New York began to set in. By end of October that year, temperatures had fallen into the forties and people were already wearing fall and winter coats. Manseh's husband did not prepare them for the changing weather, so the girls were still wearing their tropical dresses to school when everybody had made the switch to jeans, sweat pants, sweaters and coats. Manseh's husband had

started spending days at a time at his
girlfriend's house, though Manseh did not know
about it. In fact, the first week Manseh
arrived, the husband spent nights at his
girlfriend's house, but at the time, had lied to
her that he was spending those nights at the
local library because he was busy preparing for
his doctoral comprehensive examination. She had
believed him because she didn't know that people
do not sleep in the library. She had wondered
about somebody sleeping in the library, but at
the time had simply concluded that since it was
America, it could be possible, so she did not
question him about it.

It didn't take long before her children's
teachers noticed that the girls were still
dressing inappropriately for the changing
weather, so their teachers began sending notes
home to the parents. Despite the notes, the

children kept coming to school with inappropriate dresses. Manseh wanted to change her daughters' clothes, but couldn't as she did not have the means. Her husband was not available for her to discuss the children's conditions and their teachers' notes except to leave him messages on his cell phone voicemail. One day, Manseh's neighbor noticed that the younger girl was wearing a jean trouser that was very tight on her with the zipper falling apart because she had started to outgrow her pants. Her neighbor gave the little girl a brand new jean pant and a sweat shirt she had purchased for her daughter and the girl was so excited. She wore it to school the next day, and when she got to school she was so cheerful that her teacher noticed a big difference in her classroom participation and demeanor.

When their teachers asked them why they were still wearing summer clothes while the weather had turned cold, the girls told them that those were the only dresses they had, the teachers were very sorry and upset. Their teachers started a campaign in their classrooms for voluntary donation of winter clothes for the girls and the following day, the girls came home with several pairs of pants, sweaters, shirts, and even winter coats. Some of the clothes and coats fit Manseh, so she started wearing them.

Three days later, Manseh's husband came home and wanted to take the kids to Wal-Mart to purchase winter dresses for them. The kids did not want to go with him alone, so Manseh told him that she would like to accompany them, but he refused. He tried to force the girls to go with him and Manseh got in a tug-of-war with him to leave the girls alone. During the struggle, he slapped Manseh, causing her to bleed from the ear. When this was going on, the oldest girl dialed 911 and within minutes, about five police cruisers were in front of their house. That was the beginning of the end of their marriage.

Finding Shelter

After the 911 incident, the police conducted some preliminary inquiry to ascertain what happened. Following their initial inquiry, including interview with the children, they arrested Manseh's husband. From that point on, the case went to court and things began to unravel for Manseh. Not knowing how the justice system works in America, it felt like a movie to her as things began to spiral out of control. Child protective services and social services stepped in and the next thing she knew, they

were helping her obtain a restraining order from
the court against her husband.

The husband was ordered not to come close
to his house or call them. The experience was
very foreign to her as it is never done in her
country to send the man out of his home in favor
of the wife and children.

The husband had told her that he was going
to send her home, and bragged to her that as a
United States citizen, he would have her
deported. That was why he refused to file a
petition to change her status. He had reasoned
that since she did not understand the system yet
and did not have any identity or permanent
resident status, he could treat her any way he
wished and easily have her deported. Manseh kept
wondering what she and the children had done
wrong and even begged him to forgive them if
they did anything wrong. At one point, she had

started blaming herself for what was happening
to them. She even wondered why the husband
decided to bring them to America in the first
place. He could have left them where they were
because she and the children were doing fine
until he decided to bring them over to America.

Manseh's husband did everything he could to
make her life miserable. Shortly after the
courts asked him to leave the house and not to
get within 100 feet of his family, he hired a
realtor to list the house for sale. That was
designed to get the wife and kids out of his
house. After a month of Manseh refusing to
leave, mainly because she did not have any place
to go, she opened up to her next door neighbor
about what she and the girls were going through.
Her neighbor contacted some officials of her

church parish, of which she was also a member, and told them about Manseh's situation.

The parish coordinator in charge of the sanctuary program agreed to meet Manseh and her neighbor that same afternoon. After listening to Manseh's story, she concluded that it was an abuse case and decided to step in and provide them shelter. The church allowed them to stay in one of their shelters for abused and battered women on the condition that she could not tell her husband where they were staying. She and the girls gladly moved into their new home at the shelter, and she had the first good night's sleep since she arrived in America that night. A few days after Manseh and the girls moved out, her husband removed the "For Sale" sign from his house and moved back into the house with his girlfriend.

Obtaining an identity

For some inexplicable reason, Manseh's husband did not want her to have any identity. He refused to file any papers for her and the children, such as the application for a social security card or the necessary paperwork to change her immigration status. He did not want her to get a driver's license or even some police identification. He knew that she recently completed a vocational nursing program before she left for America and she begged him to help her register for the registered nurses board certification exam, but he kept delaying. In order for Manseh to register for the board exam, she had to have some identification such as a social security number.

With the help of her court-appointed lawyer and the child protective services, Manseh and her daughters were allowed to apply for social security numbers and by a court order, began the process of changing their immigration status to permanent residency. After receiving her social security number, she also obtained her driver's license with the help of a church sanctuary director who would eventually come to serve as her mentor.

Quest for Certification

Given the situation Manseh found herself in, she was advised by her neighbor to focus on preparing for the registered nurse (RN) board certification exam. During the period that she was being evicted from her husband's home, she had been contacted by her cousin who got information from home that she was now in America. It was godsend the day he called their house. She told him everything that she and her daughters were going through. Incidentally, her cousin lived about an hour's drive away from where they were, so the next day he arrived with his wife to see them. They took pity on them and told her not to despair. Manseh also told him about her desire to prepare for the RN board exam. He purchased the National Council Licensure Examination (NCLEX) for Registered Nurses practice exam software for her to practice with and got her a desktop PC. He and his wife practically moved her to her new shelter and provided them with some money for groceries.

After moving into the sanctuary home provided by the church, she embraced the church and began volunteering to help out in the church. The lady that ran the sanctuary program for the church became so impressed with her that she started helping Manseh and the kids with

money from her own pocket. She helped Manseh
register for the NCLEX exam preparatory classes
and even paid for her to take the board exam. It
took her a couple of trials and Manseh passed
the board exam. The lady from church also helped
her obtain her driver's license as well as a
fairly good used car to get back and forth to
work. Manseh would confess later that she never
knew that there were human beings in America
like the sanctuary director or her neighbor and
cousin. To her, and rightly so, these people
were the reasons she survived with her children
under the extenuating circumstances she found
herself shortly after her arrival in America, an
experience that she vowed would remain indelible
in her psyche.

Children from Venus

Manseh's story, in my opinion, is a case
study that has a divine intervention and

deserves to be told. One of the things that all parents pray and hope for is for their children to grow up adhering to and practicing the values their parents teach them. Manseh's two daughters did not only learn the good values their mother was inculcating in them, they assimilated those values. In a way, Manseh's daughters were her main backbone despite their tender ages.

Due to the hand that was dealt to Manseh, her time was almost exclusively spent with her daughters. The amount of time she spent with her children helped her weave those children into her own social life and knit herself into their lives. They in turn responded. As she would say, "They are indeed, children from Venus." Not only have the girls grown into beautiful, respectful, and helpful children, they have continued to progress academically. The older girl, who is now nineteen, has started college. She has learned to drive and Manseh bought her a car so that she could drive herself to school every day as well as take her younger sister around when she needs to. The younger girl is progressing through high school and expects to enter college in a few years.

Nurturing Good Friendships

Manseh's survival and what led to her successes resulted from the few people she came to know and the symbiotic relationships that developed. She explained that some of the things she had to do to build and nurture her friendship with the two individuals she calls her best friends were to seek their advice and keep the lines of communication open. She calls them at least once a week and also keeps in touch through brief messages left on their answering machines.

She says that she tries to always keep her
word and refrain from spreading her friends'
business. She makes sure that it is a give-and-
take relationship. She and her best friends are
there for each other through good times and bad
times. They make sure to celebrate each other's
successes, and help each other get through
failures. She also learned to be flexible with
her best friends by accepting occasional
cancellations and taking a rain check whenever
necessary.

Chapter 7:   Stuck and Forced To Stay

Except for the new generation of West African immigrants, most immigrants that came here in the 1960s, 70s, and early 80s had goals of acquiring an American education, obtaining a college degree or two and returning to their respective countries of origin with the skills necessary for the task of their nation-building. Unfortunately, corruption and mismanagement of resources by leaders of their native countries, coupled with changing global economic situations, adversely affected almost all the countries in the region, and forced many of the West African immigrants to dramatically re-evaluate their situations, and eventually altered their original objectives and goals. In a majority of cases, these West African immigrants chose to stay in America permanently.

The West African immigrants who immigrated to the United States in the last two decades are more interested in settling in America to build a better and more comfortable life for themselves and their families. An increasing number of West African immigrants today are deciding to become permanent residents and citizens of the United States instead of returning to their home countries. The reasons for this new direction of West African immigrants are beyond the scope of this book.

Temporary Protection

While many West Africans would prefer to go home; in most cases, political and economic conditions in their native countries force them to stay even if it means over staying their visas, which puts them in precarious situations in which they can only make a living working in

the underground economies earning less than
minimum wages, despite their academic
qualifications. Such was the case of Tejani
Stevens from Sierra Leone who resorted to
driving a cab, despite having a master's degree
in engineering. Stevens had been living in the
US for fifteen years. When he arrived in America
at the end of summer in 1990, he had a student
visa. In less than one year of his departure
from his home, Sierra Leone descended into a
civil war.

As the civil war escalated, it became
increasingly difficult and risky to travel
between Sierra Leone and the United States; and
by the middle of the nineties, it was almost
impossible for Sierra Leoneans to travel in and
out of their country. Many of them who had
entered the United States before the war found
themselves trapped. Suddenly, Stevens found his

status change from being a transnational to being in exile. Given that there was nothing he could do about the situation, he simply focused on his education, completing both an undergraduate degree and a master's degree by the end of 1996. In 1997, the US government granted all Sierra Leoneans living within its borders a legal status called Temporary Protected Status (TPS), which grants recipients the right to work and live in the United States legally and nothing more. At the end of each year the TPS is active, if a crisis persists in the country whose citizens were granted the TPS status, the US government can offer another year of legal status. This can potentially go on for several years, especially for those West African countries where civil wars and ethnic conflicts tend to be a chronic problem.

With the TPS, Stevens was able to legally secure a good paying job, a new car and a townhouse with a mortgage. While Stevens would have preferred to go home, he could not make the journey back because of his safety or lack thereof. He had been profoundly touched by the war in part because he had been away from his family and his culture for too long, and partly because both his parents and his only brother were killed in the civil war. He became convinced that he would have met the same fate had he not been in America. For that reason, he resolved to stay in America since there was no family to return to, but his hopes would be dashed again with an announcement in late summer of 2003 by the US Department of Homeland Security.

Sometime in October of 2003, President George W. Bush's administration decided that

since the civil war in Sierra Leone had ended,
Sierra Leoneans would no longer be covered under
the temporary protection status law, and
therefore, the Secretary of Homeland Security
gave them until May 3, 2004 to leave or be
deported. When Stevens first moved into his
house in 1999, he had legal status, a steady
job, and a mortgage. Despite everything, Stevens
was neither an American, nor on any path to
citizenship. Instead, he just found status
reversing from being an exile to a transnational
once again. He was among over 2,200 Sierra
Leoneans across the United States who had been
living and working legally in America, suddenly
facing deportation.

After many years of living a legitimate
American life, Stevens could not imagine a life
in hiding. As a law-abiding resident, Stevens

could not imagine himself living as an illegal alien. Besides, the risk of sudden deportation seemed too great. All he would have to do was slip up at work, or run afoul of the law, and he could end up in detention. He had never been so fearful and worried in his life before. So like most Sierra Leoneans who faced the likely end of their stay in America, there was little he could do about the situation except to worry and find ways to adjust his immigration status without breaking the law.

Quest for Legal Status

Stevens had been dating his girlfriend Mara for a little over five months when the news about his temporary protective status termination was announced. Mara was a US citizen of Sierra Leonean decent. Prior to November 2003, Stevens had never thought of marriage or even considered the prospect of getting married.

But after the announcement that TPS would end for Sierra Leoneans, he began entertaining the idea of getting married, should his girl friend agree. He figured that the easiest way to change his status legally was to get married to a United States citizen, and since his girlfriend Mara was a US citizen, he wouldn't mind getting married to her since they were already in an intimate relationship.

One cold winter night in December, Stevens summoned some courage and proposed to his girlfriend to marry him. After popping the question, Mara slowly began to sob and the sobbing turned into weeping. Stevens could not understand why she was crying. He felt that perhaps he had offended her and begged her to forgive him if he had done anything wrong. Suddenly, she stopped crying and quietly told him that she couldn't marry him because she was not ready for marriage, and in fact did not think she would ever get married. Stevens felt his love was unrequited. Initially he didn't think her refusal would affect their relationship, but it did. After a couple of weeks, Stevens, fearing he was running out of time, ended his relationship with Mara. His permit to work was expiring and could not be renewed again. Given the condition in which he found himself, he went underground and took up cab driving to make ends meet, forsaking his good paying job, not by choice, but because of the situation in which he found himself.

Navigating the Lonely Culture

After Tejani went underground following the expiration of his Temporary Protected Status, he felt increasingly lonely and isolated from everybody, especially from his roots. Like many

Africans, Tejani grew up in Sierra Leone and enjoyed communal living whereby members of the community shared their burden of life with one another. People watch out for each other and feel the sense of being taken care of, even when life circumstances become difficult.

But in America, and especially after losing his TPS and going underground, Tejani did not think that he had anyone with whom he could discuss his personal troubles. Unlike the community in which he grew up, he came to learn that in America, most people don't even know who their next-door neighbors are. Children are raised and encouraged to leave home, and each generation is taught to be independent and seek their own way. While this concept is not totally foreign to Tejani, what he couldn't understand was the leaving home aspect of it.

Social and Cultural Alienation

Not only did Tejani become alienated from his peers when he left the life that he was used to and took on cab driving, he also felt alienated from his roots because he had been gone for too long and no longer had a home to return to. Tejani's alienation from society was in part out of his own making. It was partly shame and partly fear of the INS that drove him to isolate himself from his community and those with similar issues who could have helped him. He felt that going from the corporate world to a life of cab driving was too humiliating for him. He stopped coming out to social events organized by members of his community and effectively alienated himself from those who could advise him on what to do.

Ironically, Tejani could not even turn to the Sierra Leone community association whose main mission was to promote the welfare of its members, especially those in need. Despite his community association's objective of offering support and advice to new immigrants from his home country, welcome them, and share their experiences, Tejani could not bring himself to face his people and share his problems with them. He simply kept to himself and went underground. Tejani became lonely, discouraged, and began feeling very much alone. His struggles with loneliness continued for months until his loneliness and discouragement turned into depression.

When his old friends heard about his problem with depression, they concluded that he was going crazy. That sent him into deeper depression. The pain became so unbearable that he contemplated few times of driving his taxi into an oncoming 18-wheeler and ending it once and for all. That's when he decided to seek help. One day, he called one of his friends, Mohamed (not his real name), whom he had not spoken to for months. When Mohamed picked up the phone, Tejani started crying. Tejani narrated his ordeal to his friend, who was himself dumbfounded because for one thing, he had not heard from Tejani for all these months and secondly, for the pathetic stories Tejani was telling him. Mohamed promised to meet him the next day. When they met, Mohamed recommended that Tejani meet with Mohamed's church counselor. After a couple of sessions, the counselor was able to convince Tejani that conquering chronic loneliness was possible, although it is an on-going process in which God plays a major role. The counselor encouraged Tejani to start attending church services every

Sunday, which he did. He started believing in God again and gradually, began to trust others who would eventually help him overcome his problems. Several years later, Tejani says that he has now found peace, except for an occasional period of loneliness. One day he came across a passage in the Bible which gave him hope and encouragement to fight on—no matter the odds:

These things I have spoken to you, that in me you may have peace. In the world you shall have trouble: but have confidence, I have overcome the world. (John 16:33)

Since he has been attending church services on a regular basis and having counseling sessions with the church counselor, Tejani now says, "I have peace and I feel safe and secure in the church." He has become a regular in the church and says that he owes his life to the church. As he put it, "If it wasn't [for] the church, I would probably be six feet under by now." He, in essence, has found comfort in the church.

Hoping For the Best

Tejani overcame his depression by finding ways to keep busy and become involved in his community again. He resolved to make a difference in someone else's life, no matter the odds and specifically in Sierra Leone. Although he had negative experiences with Sierra Leonean organizations in the past; as he put it, "Sierra Leonean and indeed, many African groups, are often a clash of egos and personalities rather than an ideal place to build a proud legacy." However, he was able to find an organization whose main purpose of existence is to support small-scale development and relief projects in Sierra Leone.

Through his contributions and others' help, his organization has made some humanitarian and social progress in Sierra Leone. Tejani's wish is to one day visit Sierra Leone to witness some of the progress he is helping bring about, but since he does not have the correct papers to leave and reenter the United States, his organization remains his only conduit to helping his people. His hope is to make the trip someday and currently, he's counting on the comprehensive immigration reform that the United States Congress and the President have been promising.

Chapter 8:   *Determined to Succeed*

The story of Tobi George is a story of sheer inventiveness and will to succeed. George was the oldest of four children born to his parents. His parents and his uncle left their native country of Togo and settled in the eastern region city of Aba, Nigeria when Tobi was three years old. While in Nigeria, his parents had three additional children (two girls and a boy). His father died when he was just eight years old, so the burden of raising George and his three siblings fell upon his mother. His mother was an elementary school auxiliary teacher (i.e., a teacher without formal teacher training) who scrounged and toiled to put him and his siblings through primary school. Primary school, which runs for six years (primary one through six), is the equivalent of elementary school in the United States. After primary school, those who wish to continue to secondary school (high school) take the Common Entrance Examination to be admitted into secondary schools.

The Burden of Being First Child

As the oldest child, George was the first to complete his primary school education and receive a first school leaving certificate, signifying the equivalent of a sixth grade education. He was a brilliant kid who wanted to go to secondary school and eventually become a university graduate. But with his father's death and his mother's meager salary as an auxiliary teacher, attaining his life-long dream became an uphill battle. George scored a distinction in his first school leaving certificate examination and when he took the Common Entrance Examination for Secondary School, he was among the top 5 percent. As a result of his performance, his mother swore to do whatever she could to put him through secondary school and possibly through college. His mother consulted her brother, who was a businessman and lived in the city of Calabar (another major city in the south eastern part of Nigeria) with his family. Her brother agreed to take George into his care. He also agreed to pay for George's way through secondary school while George's mother focused on the remaining three children. So George attended secondary school from his uncle's home and in the afternoon when he came back from school he would go to his uncle's store to help out in the business. In the process, he learned his uncle's trade. George continued to progress in secondary school with excellent grades until his fourth year.

One memorable Thursday afternoon, while George's uncle was returning from a business trip, the vehicle he was riding in was involved in a ghastly motor accident and he died at the spot. When George received the information that his uncle was dead, he had a flashback to the day that his father died. All of a sudden, he felt abandoned again. He knew immediately that his uncle's death meant the end of his secondary school education. After his uncle's death, George could no longer afford to attend secondary school. At the end of the term, with the equivalent of a tenth-grade education, George (then 16 years old) was asked to help out and run his uncle's business, so he quit school and focused on his uncle's business. He did not however, stop thinking about his education. He enrolled in a British correspondence course to help him prepare for the General Certificate of Education Ordinary Level (GCE O-Level), which is the equivalent of the West African Examination Council's School Certificate or what is popularly known as the West African School Certificate (WASC). Since he could not complete secondary school to sit for the WASC, the only alternative for him was to sit for GCE O-Level. So two years after his uncle's death, George registered for the November/December GCE O-Level. He sat for a total of six subjects, including mathematics, English, economics, chemistry, biology, and geography. When the results of the exam came out about three months later, George cleared all six subjects scoring two Alphas and four Credits (or the equivalent of two A's and four B's).

With his GCE O-Level result at hand, George began to dream again about a university

education, but the way to go about it proved to
be elusive due to financial constraints. During
this period in his difficult life, one of his
friends named Okon talked to him about the
possibility of traveling overseas to one of the
British Commonwealth nations in the Caribbean
such as Antigua. Since he grew up in Nigeria, he
practically became a Nigerian by securing a
Nigerian passport. Coming from a Commonwealth
nation, obtaining a visiting visa to Antigua
would be easier than securing a visa to the
United States or Canada. The thinking was that
if he could get to Antigua, he would then find a
way to the United States because in the 1980s it
was easier to go to the United States from
Antigua than it was from Nigeria. Given the new
scenario, George began planning his exit from
Nigeria in order to pursue his dream.

Venturing Out

With very little money in his pocket and a promise from his best friend to pay for his round trip ticket to Antigua, George set out to travel to an unknown world. He did not want too many people to know about his intended trip, just in case he did not succeed. Rather, he chose to inform only his mother, his siblings, and his uncle's wife. Initially his uncle's wife did not like the idea because if George left, she would have to find another reliable person to run her dead husband's business. It was purely based on selfish reasons that she resisted it; but after George explained to her why he had to seek a way out of the situation in which he found himself, she came to see that there was not much advancement for him in the business. With that hurdle out of the way, George was literally cleared to leave home.

George's best friend's parents were so
affluent that his friend could afford a round
trip ticket to Antigua five times if he wanted
to. He promised to pay the round trip ticket for
both of them with the understanding that someday
George will pay him back. Okon, his friend also
made the arrangement to travel to Antigua with
the agent who was responsible for securing visas
for the would-be travelers. One of the
requirements for obtaining a visa to Antigua is
that the traveler must have a round-trip airline
ticket and a valid passport. So, George secured
for himself a valid Nigerian passport and handed
it over to his friend to obtain the flight
tickets and the visas. About two weeks later,
his friend came back with a round trip ticket
and George's passport with visa to Antigua.

On the departure date, George and his friend traveled to Lagos for a rendezvous with their agent who was supposed to travel with them to Antigua & Barbuda. On the scheduled departure date, they left on a British Airways flight via London and after almost two day's journey, they arrived at the V.C. Bird International Airport in Antigua. After going through customs with no problems whatsoever, George and his entourage caught a taxi to the Admiral's Inn located in St. John's. The next day, their agent took them to the private university where they registered for classes. One of the conditions for them to remain on the island for some extended period of time was to be registered in a school or be on a business trip. After registering them for classes, the agent collected the return tickets from George and his friend and told them that he would keep the tickets for them. However, two

days later, the agent left the island of Antigua
with their return tickets and flew back to
Lagos. As they were to find out later, the agent
eventually redeemed the tickets.

After the agent disappeared with their
return tickets, George felt abandoned once more.
This was the third time in his young life that
he felt abandoned—the first was when his father
passed away, and the second was when his uncle
was killed in a car accident. This time around,
it was in a foreign country, thousands of miles
away from home. George cried and moped around
for three days. Finally, he gathered himself
together, remembering that he was the first
child of his parents and that his family was
looking up to him. He summoned the courage to
find a way to work himself out of Antigua.

Searching for a way out

Once it became clear to George that he had been abandoned by his trip coordinator, he went into a survival mode. Luckily, his friend still had a reasonable amount of money such that if they were frugal enough, they could stay in Antigua for at least nine months without working. With the little amount of money he had, he reasoned that he would have to find a job in Antigua in order to survive. He convinced his friend that they needed to move out of the inn where they had been staying and find a place where they could share accommodation with other people. So, the first thing George set out to do was to get familiar with the island. He got himself a good map of Antigua and studied it very carefully.

In Antigua, renting a car was the ideal way to discover more of the island. George and his friend set out to explore the Island by renting

a car for one day at a cost of $30 per day. In

order to drive in Antigua, he needed a valid

driver's license from his country of residence,

or an international driver's license and a

permit to drive in Antigua. Although George did

not have a valid driver's license, his friend

did. For about $15, the rental agency assisted

them in getting the temporary license, which was

valid for three months. The first adjustment his

friend had to make was to learn how to drive on

the left side of the road in a car that also had

its steering on the left hand side. After a

couple of miles on the road, George's friend got

used to Antigua driving and they went on to

explore the island.

After one day of driving around the island,

George and his best friend came to know more

about Antigua. They even discovered potential areas to live and perhaps work. George and his friend began mapping out where to seek employment to supplement their funds. At the time, the easiest job to get was as a security guard. George and his best friend approached a car dealership for security guard positions. In a couple of days, they both got jobs working the night-shift.

While working as security guard and going to school, George and his friend began planning their exit from Antigua. Their ultimate destination was, of course, the United States. But to exit, they needed enough money to pay their way out by getting to know some natives and eventually securing Antiguan passports. This meant that they had to work for a period of time to accumulate funds while familiarizing themselves with some of the natives. Their travel to the United States depended, to a large

extent, on knowing the right people who could

help them obtain Antiguan passports.

After nine months in Antigua, George and

his friend's exit plans were taking shape. They

had made solid arrangements for obtaining

Antiguan passports, which would make it easier

for them to travel to Canada. George's friend

was the first to exit as his own passport became

ready a couple of weeks after their ninth month

in Antigua. George had to wait for two more

months for his passport to become available. By

the time George left Antigua, his best friend

had been gone for three months.

George's trip to the United States was not

direct. He had to go through Canada partly

because his best friend had decided to settle in

Canada and partly because as a Commonwealth

nation, Antiguan citizens could travel to Canada without visas. So about one year after he arrived in Antigua, George landed in Canada, a stone's throw away from his dream destination. A couple of weeks later, one of his family friends from Nigeria who lived in New York City drove his taxi from New York to Toronto to pick him up and drive him into New York City. George arrived in New York, eager to live the American dream. Little did he know that his struggle was just about to begin.

American Adventure

When George arrived in New York he lived with his friend whom he calls Freddie in a studio apartment in Bronx, New York. It was Freddie who had driven George into New York from Canada in his taxi cab. George wasted no time in asking for where and how to secure a job. Freddie explained to him that the only job he could find would have to be a job where he would be paid under the table.

In New York City, one could pretty much do any job for cash. Being a city sprawling with immigrants, New York City is extremely popular with foreign workers that do not have any visas or work papers, so finding such a job was easy as long as he was willing and able to work. Jobs such as dishwashing in restaurants, babysitting, housekeeping, warehousing, and construction can be found for under-the-table arrangements. For George, that meant relief because he was eager and willing to work, doing any work that could help him take care of himself and hopefully, allow him to take college courses to improve himself as well.

Working under the Table

One day after his arrival in New York City, George took a stroll around their neighborhood after Freddie went to work. By that evening when Freddie came back from work, George had discovered some of the neighborhood supermarkets and grocery stores as potential places to look for work. He was however, disappointed after approaching about five establishments and being turned down by each one. When Freddie came home that evening, George told him about his experience. Freddie explained to him that under-the-table jobs are often easier to land from small businesses, where the boss is the owner, and is prepared to take the risks that big companies would not take. He explained to him that the key to landing such jobs is to inquire at the corner stores instead of supermarkets.

Freddie promised to take him around. Later that evening, Freddie escorted George to make inquiries at businesses that he was sure of. Their first stop was at a fabrics warehouse, but the owner said that he was not in need of any help. Their second stop was a grocery store and to George's amazement, the owner asked him to start work the next morning in the meat section to load and unload meat from the storage freezer or meat cooler for $5.50 an hour. He was to be paid cash every Friday and was to work as long as needed. George was so excited about the offer that he forgot to find out the conditions of the job. The first day at work George almost froze to death because he did not wear the proper clothing for the meat cooler. However, when he went back to work the second day, he was wearing a heavy coat even though it was the middle of the summer season. George worked from 7:00 AM

till 7:00 PM with 1 hour break for lunch and

short breaks, Monday through Saturday.

While the job was tedious, George never

complained. In fact, he was so happy to be

working and getting paid every Friday that he

never skipped a single day of work for 6 months.

His employer became so impressed with his hard

work and dedication that he increased his pay to

$6.00 an hour after 6 months, and asked him to

take a day off.

Eating Lunch just for the Rich

During his first week on the job, George

was spending $1.00 on a hamburger for lunch.

When Freddie found out that George was buying

lunch every day, he confronted George and

accused him of being extravagant. Freddie told

George that buying lunch was only for the rich

people. He advised George that he ought to be

thinking about how to be sending money to his

poor mother he left at home. George did not need

to be reminded that he was poor or that he had

many responsibilities back home, especially as

the oldest child and first son of his parents.

In his own mind, going to school to improve his

skills and chances was more important. So to

make peace with Freddie, he promised not to eat

lunch again.

George kept his word to stop eating lunch.

However, after three days of no lunch, he

discovered a better way of saving money without

starving himself to death. He would simply

purchase a loaf of bread for less than $1.00,

some bologna and a jar of peanut butter. Every

morning he would make himself a bologna-peanut

butter sandwich and took it to work for lunch.

He realized that for less than $5.00 he could

eat lunch for a week. With the lunch issue

behind him, he began thinking about how to get

back to school to improve his skills.

Obtaining Education through the Back Door

George had been asking questions on how to

go about obtaining his GED since he could not

use his General Certificate of Education

Ordinary Level to secure admission without being

discovered as an out-of-state or illegal

immigrant. He found out where to go and register

for his GED and how to prepare for it. For three

months, he spent every night after work

preparing for the GED exam. At the end of three

months, he took the GED exam without any

difficulty. His next move was to gain admission

in a two-year college for an associate degree

program. Not long after George received his GED,

he applied for and obtained admission to study

computer electronics in one of the two-year colleges in Manhattan.

George attended night school while working during the day to make ends meet. Between attending classes and doing what seemed to be an unending series of homework and preparation for quizzes and tests, George barely got four hours of sleep every night. Sleep deprivation became a major struggle for him. While George did everything he could to stay healthy because he did not have health insurance, he did not know the detrimental effects his sleep deprivation was having on his health. For example, he observed that since he started using the subway to go to class he had been catching cold viruses more frequently than he used to. He also noticed that his coordination was not what it used to be

while at work. He became even more worried about
making a mistake at work and losing his job.

Two and one-half years later, George
graduated from the two-year college, receiving
an Associate degree in computer electronics.
After graduation, George spent the next full
week sleeping from the time he came home from
work till 6:00 AM the following morning. Just
about one month after receiving his diploma,
George decided to enlist in the Army. He went
down to the US Army recruitment office one day
and few weeks later, he was in Fort Leonard
Wood, Waynesville, Missouri for US Army basic
training to become a combat engineer.

While George knew that army boot camp would
last about nine weeks with marching, drill,
ceremonies, and lots of standing in formation,
he did not really know what he was getting
himself into until he arrived at the boot camp.

With the type of work George did—heavy lifting of frozen meat, George thought that he would have no problem with the physical aspect of the training, but he came to discover that no matter how fit he thought he was, the drills pushed him to the point of muscle failure. Nine weeks later, he graduated from boot camp and went on to complete the advanced individual training (job training). George completed his first tour of duty (four years) and re-enlisted for another four years. While enlisted, he took advantage of technology advancements that have enabled people, including American service men and women all over the world to pursue their educational dreams through online universities. He has since completed his bachelor's degree, became a commissioned officer and got married. At the time of the book's publication, he was in his

12th year of active duty, a United States Army

Captain and a naturalized US citizen.

Chapter 9:   *Other hurdles for West African Immigrants*

Homelessness

Many West African immigrants sometimes become homeless or at least come close to it when they first arrive in America. Sometimes, the experiences are so traumatic and frightening that they internalize them and pretend not to remember. For somebody like Festus Wale, when he finally reached Rochester, New York on a Labor Day weekend and could not find anyone to help him find a place to stay, he panicked and eventually wound up in a YMCA building downtown Rochester. He was afraid to eat or buy anything other than his bus pass and snacks for nourishment until three weeks later when one of his brother's friends came and took him to his house.

Constant Harassments by the INS

In the eighties and nineties, it seemed as though the INS agents had it in for Africans. Stopping Africans in public places to ascertain their legality was a routine practice for the INS agents. Consider the story of James Omar, another West African. One summer afternoon Omar went to downtown Buffalo to the Greyhound Bus station to pick up some friends that had arrived from Rochester. During the summer season, many West Africans enjoy wearing their African attire because of the hot weather. On that eventful summer afternoon, many African students were also wearing their traditional attire and many were downtown at the bus station. Sure enough, INS agents were scouring the bus station looking for Africans. It seemed like racial profiling pure and simple. It had to be because all they did was stop you if you were wearing African

attire or if you were Black and had a foreign
accent.

On that day, Omar picked up his friends and
there were two other West African women with
them. As soon as they came out of the bus
station, two INS gentlemen approached them and
identified themselves as INS agents. The agents
then asked them for their identification.
Fortunately, Omar had his student identification
in his wallet so he presented it. They were not
satisfied and had to call his school to confirm
that he was registered there. The women did not
have their identification on them and therefore
were carted away to the INS holding facility
downtown. Their husbands, who were at the time
doctoral students at SUNY Buffalo, had to go
downtown where their wives were being held to

prove their legality and get them out of detention.

Professorial Victimization

Many African students believe that some of their college professors assume at the outset that African students cannot compete academically with their American counterparts. For that reason, for an African to earn a grade of A in a class, he or she would have to perform above and beyond his/her American counterparts. That means putting extra effort (110%) to earn the points necessary to score good grades for courses. In my opinion, many African students learn about this unspoken practice early in their college experiences allowing them to adjust their tactics, however, a lot of them find out too late.

Consider the story of Adrianne Anayo, a West African, and a former nursing student at the University Of Maryland School Of Nursing. On one occasion, one of her instructors handed out an assignment that would require some research and a write-up. There were only two African students in that class, Anayo and another lady, who was also from West Africa. After handing out the assignments, the instructor said, "I don't want to read any accents in the paper." When she made that comment, Anayo interjected and asked her to clarify what she meant by her statement. The professor became very defensive. How does one read an accent in an essay? The truth is that most West African immigrants (especially those that come from English-speaking countries where English is the official language) have a better command of grammar than their American counterparts. Yet, many instructors have this false notion that West Africans can't write English or communicate very well.

Or consider the case of J.T. Williams, another West African who lived and studied in New York. According to Williams, some of his professors were helpful and understanding, while most of them were ignorant and mean. Williams told a story about his English professor, who thought that he had help writing an in-class essay because, according to his professor, "a foreign student with an accent should not be able to write with such a good command of English language without help from a second party." Williams' professor made him retake the test for him to believe that Williams was good enough to write as well as he did.

After Williams retook the test, his professor was compelled to read the essay to the whole class because it was so well-done. It is fair to report that today, Williams is a

successful practicing attorney in both the state

of Maryland and the District of Columbia

(Washington DC).

PART III: WEST AFRICANS AND THE IMMIGRATION DEBATE

"Love the family you're given, but gather the family you need"
(Author Unknown)

Chapter 10:   Taking Aim at the Immigration Debate

The Debate

In January of 2004, President George W. Bush proposed a variety of immigration law reforms to the United States Congress in the form of a statement of principles, rather than legislation. He urged Congress to pass comprehensive immigration reform legislation.

By the end of March 2006, a debate had erupted in the United States over the prospect of new laws to criminalize undocumented immigrants and those who support them. Senators Edward Kennedy and John McCain crafted and passed a bill that had all the elements the President had proposed, but then the bill was stalled in the House of Representatives and

eventually died a natural death of never
becoming law.

In response to the proposed legislation,
which would have raised penalties for illegal
immigration and classify illegal immigrants and
anyone who helped them enter or remain in the US
as felons, millions of people joined in protests
all over the country. And as part of the wider
immigration debate, most of the protests not
only sought a rejection of the bill, but also a
comprehensive reform of the country's
immigration laws that included a path to
citizenship for all undocumented immigrants.
While the immigration bill did not become law,
the problem of illegal immigration did not go
away.

On May 17, 2007, another plan that would
grant legal status to illegal immigrants and
increase border and interior enforcement

initiatives was announced by some Senators and the White House. While nobody really knows the exact number of illegal immigrants in the United States, the official estimate puts the number at nearly 11 million. According to research conducted in March of 2004 by the Pew Hispanic Center, of the estimated 11 million illegal immigrants in the United States, 5.9 million (57%) are of Mexican origin, 2.5 million (24%) are from other Latin-American countries, 1.0 million (9%) are of Asian origin, 0.6 million (6%) are of European and Canadian origin, and 0.4 million (4%) are of African origin[10]. The issue is how to handle the 11 million that are here illegally and make them legal, law-abiding residents without appearing to encourage illegal

---

[10] Jeffrey S. Passel, "Estimates of the Size and Characteristics of the Undocumented Population," Pew Hispanic Center Report, March 21, 2005.

immigration. Again, the effort died in Congress without any solution to the immigration problem.

In April 2010, the debate over immigration reform was again rekindled when the Arizona State legislature passed a new anti-immigration law and the Arizona governor, Jan Brewer, signed what has been perceived by most people as "the nation's strictest law against illegal immigrants."[11] The law requires local and state police to question people about their immigration status if there is reason to believe they are in the country illegally, which makes it a state crime to be in the United States illegally. The law also requires that immigration-status questions would follow a law enforcement officer's stopping, detaining, or arresting a person while enforcing another law.

---

[11] Randal C. Archibold, "Arizona Enacts Stringent Law on Immigration," *New York Times*, April 23, 2010.

Almost immediately, tens of thousands of people in cities across the United States joined protests against the controversial Arizona anti-immigration law, calling on Congress and President Barack Obama to reform the nation's immigration system. What is interesting to note is that four years earlier, more than a million people across the country united to protest the federal legislation that would have made being an illegal immigrant a felony. The movement had maintained an annual May 1st immigration reform rally. The movement, however, had been fractured and the annual May 1st rally attendance dropped sharply as attempts to reform federal immigration policy fizzled. Of the 2010 immigration reform protests, probably the biggest one took place in Los Angeles, where officials estimated some 60,000[12] people were marching downtown compared to the 2006 protests in which about one million people marched for a similar rally in the city.

Paying the Price

There is no question that most West Africans that immigrate to the United States go through the legal channels with the proper papers and, as a result, are documented. While some of them end up over staying their visas, the total number that do so is insignificant. Yet, based on the way the US Immigration and Customs Enforcement (ICE) deals with Africans and particularly West Africans, one would think that they are the largest culprits of illegal immigration to the United States. The truth lies in the numbers. The same Pew Hispanic Center study conducted in March of 2004 shows that the

---

[12] Rob Woollard, "Thousands March in US May Day Immigration Protests". Agence France-Presse (May 1,

number of visa over stayers varies considerably from country to country. In fact, of the top ten countries with the largest number of over stayers, only South Africa was an African country that made the list with 2,300 South African over stayers in the United States. As a matter of fact, of the estimated 11.1 million unauthorized immigrants in the U.S., African nations and other nations together contribute only 3% or about 400,000 illegal immigrants in the United States.

However, when the papers of these Africans expire, they focus mostly on making themselves legal again and as a result they never make noise or participate in civil disobedience such as the marching of illegal immigrants across the country demanding recognition and a path to citizenship. In most cases, they shy away from such public pronouncements because if they do speak up, they would most certainly be rounded up by immigration authorities and sent home as there are rarely any groups that lobby on their behalf when it comes to immigration matters.

The reality is that while there are adequate, enforceable laws on the books to check illegal and unauthorized immigration to the United States, those who are supposed to enforce the laws would rather apply the laws to Africans than focus on those immigrants from countries that contribute the vast majority of illegal immigrants to this country. Usually when these immigration laws are passed the target is often Mexicans, Central and South Americans. However, after enactment, their enforcement is often against Africans—especially the West African unauthorized immigrants—simply because they do not have lobbyists looking after their interests as other immigrant groups do.

Likely Consequences of the Proposed Law

While both sides of the immigration debate have tried to convince the American people why the proposed immigration law is either good or bad for America, all of them have focused only on their own areas of interest. But the most likely unintended consequence of these proposed laws is the "brain drain" effect that it will have on those countries whose citizens would like to come to America; and in the long run, create more dependency on America, resulting in more illegal immigration. Let's take a look at why this will be so.

In the seventies and eighties, many West Africans came to America to study and a majority of them would often return to their home countries at the end of their studies. Many of them did not have college education when they immigrated. They simply came to America to be college educated and eventually returned to their home countries to take up jobs that were being handled by expatriates. Those who wanted to immigrate to America were fewer because not many people had the financial resources to go to America to study. It wasn't until the mid-eighties, when corrupt leaders of most of the West African countries began running their economies down, that many of the immigrant students began to over stay and seek long-term residency rather than go back to their home countries. It could be proven that when a nation's political and economic system is stable, fewer of its citizens emigrate. That will be a topic for another book.

In the nineties, most West Africans that came to America emigrated as university graduates seeking jobs and better lives for their families. Making immigration based on educational background of the immigrants would simply create a massive exodus of the people that are supposed to help stabilize those countries. This, in turn, will make those countries even more dependent on the United States and consequently create more illegal immigration. What many fail to understand is that the United States is seen as the place "where the food is."

When you have a bunch of hungry people and you lock up food in a warehouse, the hungry will always find a way to get to the food even if it costs them their lives. As long as America is seen by the developing world as the land where the food is, immigrants will always flock to America, even if it means crossing American borders illegally at the expense of their lives.

If America is serious about curtailing immigration particularly illegal immigration, its immigration policies and laws must be geared towards economic stabilization of those countries from which illegal immigrants come, instead of encouraging them to leave. A case in point is Canada, America's closest neighbor to the north. The reason that Canadians do not emigrate illegally to the United States is because Canada has a stable economy and as a result, Canadian citizens do not see any need to rush to America, either legally or illegally. However, if you live in a country where corrupt leaders loot the country's resources, run the economy down to the point that inflation and unemployment are rampant, and you have some education and you are given a choice to go to America based on your educational attainment, making the decision to leave will not be difficult.

The negative aspects of the brain drain that this policy will bring include the loss of human capital, resulting in shortages in critical sectors like health, education, public services, industry, and science as well as a loss of national economic investment and tax revenue. Brain drain will reduce the already low quantity of skilled manpower available in African countries and needed for their development. It will reduce numbers of dynamic and innovative people, whether entrepreneurs or academics. It will increase dependence on foreign technical assistance, slow the transfer of technology and widen the gap between African and industrialized countries. It will negatively affect the continent's scientific output. Money will be lost in income tax revenues and in potential contributions to gross domestic product of the losing countries.

Not everything about the measure will be negative, though. There are also positive sides like remittances, transfers of knowledge and technology, and contribution of new skills when and if migrants return. Remittances from skilled migrants will boost household welfare and support the balance of payments. However, the negative impact outweighs the positive. While it is assumed that migrants will return, resulting in transfers of knowledge and technology with new skills; in practice, they often do not return. Those that do return do so when they have reached retirement age with little or no input to the development of their nations.

Solving the Immigration Issue

In order to solve the illegal immigration issue in the United States, the two political parties (Republicans and Democrats) must lower their rhetoric and face the issue realistically. From an immigrant's point of view, I believe the following must be done to solve the immigration issue once and for all.

Current undocumented immigrants working in the country will have to be granted temporary-worker status (work permit) for five years.

Employers must be required to use e-Verify to check the legal work status of all potential employees or face consequences in terms of high fines up to $5000 per incident, and/or jail time. The undocumented immigrant worker will then get to pay taxes for the services they enjoy. At the end of the five years, the temporary-worker status will expire and the undocumented worker will no longer be in the e-Verify system.

However, ninety days before the end of the five-year work permit, the undocumented immigrants who participated successfully in the five-year temporary worker program as law-abiding and productive members of their communities would have to apply for permanent residence status.

At the end of the five-year temporary worker status period, the undocumented immigrants must then leave the country after submitting their application for green card and go back to their home countries to wait for their interview dates. Those who apply for permanent resident status at the end of the five-year temporary worker status period, voluntarily leave the country, and are eligible, will certainly be invited for an interview for permanent resident status within one to two years.

The other aspect of the immigration issue deals with border control. The federal government will be required to bolster the US Border Patrol by placing officers in visible spots to deter those considering crossing the border. In addition, walls will have to be constructed in those portions of the border that are considered most dangerous. This will ensure that would-be illegal immigrants will not attempt to cross the border by using the dangerous parts of the border in an attempt to avoid the visible border patrol agents.

This approach to the illegal immigration problem covers all three aspects of the immigration issue. First, the humanitarian aspect of the debate is addressed by allowing undocumented workers a five-year work permit. Second, the legal enforcement angle is dealt with by requiring employers to verify potential employees' legal work status or face consequences. Finally, the border control aspect is handled by building walls along the most dangerous portions of the border and lining up the remaining parts of the border with visible border patrol agents.

Some may argue that sending people back to their home countries to wait one to two years for permanent resident status is harsh, as some of the illegal immigrants would most likely have family members whose education or careers would be interrupted. However, that's a small price to pay for entering the country illegally in the first place. Besides, there are illegal immigrants today that are being sent back to their home countries to wait for one to two years and sometimes longer, before rejoining their families.

Some might also argue that undocumented immigrants may not make their presence known. However, that would be foolish on the part of the undocumented immigrants because if they do not step forward voluntarily, they will have only themselves to blame. After five years, undocumented immigrants will no longer be available in e-Verify and employers will no longer be able to verify their legal status thereby preventing them from getting hired because of the hefty penalties employers would be subjected to if they knowingly hired unverifiable, illegal immigrants.

Some states including Arizona, Mississippi, and Alabama have recently passed anti-illegal immigration laws requiring e-Verification. For example, the new Mississippi law which is called, "Mississippi Employment Protection Act", among other things requires that all new hires be e-verified on a Department of Homeland Security database making it a felony to work without authorization in the state.

On the other hand, if the undocumented and illegal immigrants come out and accept the five-year temporary worker status, after five years of legal status and a one to two-year absence from the country, they would become eligible for permanent resident status, which will then put them on a path towards citizenship.

The issue of illegal immigration always evokes strong passion on all sides of the immigration debate, but unless the issue is dealt with realistically and humanely, the problem is bound to linger and grow. If the debate continues the way it has been, the approaches espoused by each side of the debate would be irreconcilable, perpetuating the problem. The way to solve the stalemate is for the executive branch and Congressional leaders to take elements that are essential and workable (such as the ideas discussed above) and craft viable legislation that can be supported by both parties, and begin the healing process as well as the ultimate resolution of the immigration problem. The immigration issue will continue to cast a shadow over this country and will not go away unless it is dealt with. Also, it cannot be resolved on one side's argument no matter how much each side tries to demagogue the issue. The only way to resolve it is through compromise, period.

Chapter 11: Impact of 9/11 on West African Immigrants

New Fears of the West African Immigrant

A 2004 report by the Washington-based Migration Policy Institute, which relied on data from the State Department, stated that the United States resettles more refugees than any other nation. But, after the bombing of the World Trade Center in New York City on September 11, 2001, the number of refugees allowed by United States into the country fell from 112,811 in 1991 to 28,455 in 2003[13].

Prior to the 9/11 attacks, the federal refugee program had just begun to change its focus from Cold War sources to the resettlement of people who were more likely to be "real" refugees. After the attacks, the refugee program's shift to the Middle East and Africa with an increase in Muslim refugees, became a problem. Newly-mandated screening procedures became costly and took time to implement. Refugee admissions to the

United States for 2002 dropped to 27,000, the lowest number in twenty-five years. Background checks on refugees intensified, resulting in a reduction of the number of refugees allowed in. And once in the United States, groups of refugees were treated differently, depending on their country of origin.

Missed Opportunity

Shortly after the attack on the twin towers in New York on September 11, 2001 (a day that the world will forever remember as 9/11), the entire free world sympathized with the United

---

[13] Erin Patrick, "The US Refugee Resettlement Program," Migration Policy Institute (June 2004),

States and almost every nation rallied around the United States to condemn the unprovoked, unimaginable act of using commercial passenger planes to bring down the World Trade Center buildings, killing thousands of innocent people.

Based on that support, America had the greatest opportunity ever to deal a blow to terrorism once and for all. Three days later, when the then-President, George W. Bush stood alongside a firefighter atop the ash-covered remains of a fire truck, using a megaphone to announce to the world that those who committed the unspeakable act and those harboring them would soon hear from the United States, my thought was that we were really going to deal with those terrorists and their backers once and for all. A few days later, it was determined that Osama Bin Laden and the al Qaeda terror network committed the act and that the Taliban, who were in control of Afghanistan at the time, harbored them. Based on that revelation and our President's remarks, I came to the conclusion that President Bush was going to do a "Truman" on al Qaeda and the Taliban in Afghanistan, though without the atom bomb.

What do I mean by doing a "Truman" on al Qaeda and the Taliban one might ask? On July 30, 1945, President Harry S. Truman approved the bombing of Hiroshima with the atom bomb and on August 6 1945, a US B-29 Super fortress bomber named "Enola Gay" dropped an atomic bomb which exploded about 602 yards (550 meters) over the city of Hiroshima, producing the equivalent of fifteen kilotons of energy and obliterating about 81 percent of the city. Three days later, a second atomic bomb, originally destined for Kokura on the southern Japanese island of

Kyushu, was dropped on the secondary target of the shipyards of Nagasaki due to cloud cover.

The Nagasaki bomb produced about 20 kilotons of energy, but did less damage because of the local topography. It exploded above Urakami to the north of the port, destroying about 50 percent of the city. On August 15, six days after the bombing of Nagasaki, Japan surrendered to the Allied Powers, and signed the Instrument of Surrender on September 2, officially ending the Pacific War and effectively ending World War II.

The thinking behind the usage of the atom bomb was to unleash an unimaginable level of force to disrupt and demoralize the enemy into unconditional surrender. The principle was stated clearly by the then-Secretary of War, Henry Stimson. In his memoirs, Henry Stimson described the deliberate policy of overwhelming

shock:

> "I felt that to extract a genuine surrender
> from the Emperor and his military advisers,
> there must be administered a tremendous
> shock which would carry convincing proof of
> our power to destroy the empire. Such an
> effective shock would save many times the
> number of lives, both American and
> Japanese, than it would cost".[14]

One could argue that this was what happened

on August 14 when Emperor Hirohito declared his

capitulation to the Japanese people and, on

August 15, Japan announced her intention to

surrender to the Allied Powers.

Applying the same Truman principle to the

Taliban in Afghanistan without the use of atomic

bombs was what I thought President Bush and his

military advisers were going to do. The United

States had the right and support of the world

and would have been justified to defend itself

against an unprovoked attack by al Qaeda and the Taliban. Without going into intelligence, there is no question that the United States has different types of non-nuclear, conventional bombs that could have been used effectively on Afghanistan to achieve results similar to that of Japan without the radiation effect that accounted for more than half of the Japanese casualties. To my greatest surprise and dismay, we took a different course of action against Afghanistan and later invaded Iraq, which in my opinion, emboldened the terrorists and eventually brought us the proliferation of al Qaeda in places like Iraq, Afghanistan, Pakistan, Yemen, Somalia, and Europe, as well as the shoe bomber, the Christmas day bomber, and other al Qaeda-like terrorist groups including *Boko Haram* (which means "Western education is a

---

[14] Henry L. Stimson, "The Decision to Use the Atomic Bomb", *Bulletin of the Atomic Scientists*, Feb 1947, Vol. 3, No. 2: 32

sin[15]"), a Northern Nigerian Islamist group that seeks the imposition of Sharia law in the northern states of Nigeria.

It was truly a missed opportunity on the part of the United States and President George W. Bush to deal with radical Muslim terrorism once and for all. Just as Truman's decision to use the atom bomb on Japan ended the Second World War and ushered in more than fifty years of non-aggression from Japan, Bush could have used a similar massive force without the atom bomb to address radical Muslim terrorism perhaps for the next fifty-plus years.

What United States Needed To Do

Shortly after the 9/11 attack, President Bush appeared to have settled on a new principle that the United States had the right to secure

---

[15] Toni Johnson, Council on Foreign Relations, "Boko Haram", December 27, 2011.

itself against countries that harbor or give aid
to terrorist groups. In his address to the
nation that evening of September 11, 2001, the
President stated his resolution by declaring
that "we will make no distinction between the
terrorists who committed these acts and those
who harbor them."[16] The principle seemed to be
specific and targeted at those who commit
terrorist acts against the United States and
those who harbor or provide support to them. The
President went on to make an even more
aggressive restatement of the principle in his
September 20, 2001 address to a Joint Session of
Congress:

> We will pursue nations that provide aid or
> safe haven to terrorism. Every nation, in
> every region, now has a decision to make.
> Either you are with us, or you are with the
> terrorists. From this day forward, any
> nation that continues to harbor or support

---

http://www.cfr.org/africa/boko-haram/p25739.
[16] George W. Bush, "Statement by the President in His Address to the Nation," *The White House*, September 11, 2001, http://georgewbush-whitehouse.archives.gov/news/releases/2001/09/print/20010911-16.html.

terrorism will be regarded by the United States as a hostile regime.[17]

Armed with the new principle of making no distinction between terrorists who commit terror acts against the United States and those who harbor them, the President should have given the Taliban seventy-two hours to produce Osama Bin Laden and his lieutenants or face the full wrath of the United States' military power, a true "shock and awe" never seen before. After seventy-two hours and if the Taliban did not produce Osama Bin Laden and his lieutenants, send down 80 to 100 B-1 and B-52 bombers, each armed with two 5,000 or 10,000 pound bombs, pick the first city of high military importance to Afghanistan and level it. After the destruction of the first city, issue another demand to the

---

[17] George W. Bush, "Address to a Joint Session of Congress and the American People," *The White House*, September 20, 2001, http://georgewbush-whitehouse.archives.gov/news/releases/2001/09/print/20010920-8.html.

Taliban to produce Osama Bin Laden and his lieutenants in forty-eight hours. If they failed to do so, send down another batch of bombers, pick the next city and flatten it.

After the first two cities were destroyed, it would have become abundantly clear to the Taliban that the United States meant business and should not be toyed with. In addition, any nation that lets the terrorists in will face the same wrath from the United States.

Just like Emperor Hirohito and his military advisers capitulated after Hiroshima and Nagasaki bombing, the Taliban and their supporters would have also capitulated and handed Osama Bin Laden over.

Pakistan would not have allowed them to resettle in their land for fear of facing the same wrath as Afghanistan and no nation would have dared to allow them in. All the new energy that the terrorists have today would not have happened because no nation would have allowed them to operate from their soil. The shoe bomber or the underwear bomber incidents would never have happened and none of these ragtag terror groups like Boko Haram in Nigeria would have sprung up.

What To Do Next Time

Perhaps, the exact tactics used by al Qaeda to bring down the twin towers may never be used again, but al Qaeda is determined and emboldened to inflict damage on the United States and its interests. It is not a matter of if they will strike again; it is a matter of when and how. So, it is important that the President (and his or her military advisers) who will face the next successful attack by the terrorists, take the proper steps to revenge and deter once and for all, any more attacks from would-be terrorists. President Bush already established the principle of no distinction between terrorists who attack the United States interests and those who harbor them; therefore, the next President that faces such attacks must make sure that the attackers and their backers are severely punished beyond reason so as to deter future planners of terror.

Possible Criticisms

There is no question that the principle announced by President Bush resulted in criticisms and controversy. The actions enunciated in this book would have caused even more controversy. Some would have argued that a lot of innocent civilians would have been killed. There is no doubt that a lot of casualties would have resulted from the bombings. But when you consider all the casualties thus far from the Afghanistan and

Iraq wars, all the money spent so far and the quagmire United States and its allies have gotten themselves into in Afghanistan and Iraq, the number of casualties and resources spent would have been limited compared to what we have now. In other words, more lives would have been saved and fewer resources would have been spent. Instead of still debating on when and how to exit from Afghanistan and Iraq, the debate would have been about whether or not the United States used too much force, but the problem would have been taken care of quicker and cheaper.

Impact on West African Immigrants

Following the 9/11 attack, the impact on West African immigration to the United States was very dramatic -- the number of immigrants from Western Africa fell sharply. More than ten years after the attack and the resulting wars, although the number of West African immigrants to the United States has steadily improved, the number is still relatively down compared to years preceding the attack. That number is unlikely to go up anytime soon based on other developments resulting from the Iraq war including the attempt by a West African to bring down an Airliner over Detroit on Christmas Day in 2009.

Since the start of the Iraq war, al Qaeda has made many efforts to recruit West African Muslim youths to fight their self-declared Jihad War against the West. Despite al Qaeda's concerted efforts to recruit West Africans, they have been unsuccessful until the recruitment of Umar Farouk Abdulmutallab, the so called "2009 Christmas Day Bomber" or "Underwear Bomber" from Nigeria. The reason for their unsuccessful campaign thus far is because most West Africans, and Nigerians in particular, are not interested in dying as martyrs for somebody else's warped causes; but rather, are more interested in improving their lives and eradicating the poverty that plagues their communities. Culturally, Nigerians see death as a defeat of destinies. If a Nigerian dies at a very young age (less than 70 years old), it is considered to be untimely and thus a stigma that could affect the status of such a family as other families tend to avoid marriage relationships with the one who loses its members untimely.

Culturally, the Nigerian by nature does not commit suicide. Because of the high social and communal collateral culture imposes on Nigerians, a Nigerian who attempts or commits suicide brings shame to his or her family for life. A person that commits suicide cannot be buried by his or her kinsmen, only outsiders can bury such a person. A case in point is a Nigerian named Mathias who after several years of struggling to complete his bachelors and masters degrees from SUNY Brockport in the late 80s, jumped into the Genesee River in Rochester New York and drowned. He committed suicide because he had immigration problems. When his body was discovered seven days later, members of the Nigerian Community rallied around to send his corpse home to Nigeria. However, when his family was contacted, they asked the Nigerian Community not to bother sending his body home, simply because he committed suicide. Nigerians don't like to marry into such a family with history of suicide as they believe that it could be hereditary. Even the very few (less than 1 percent) who are engaged in criminal activities are only interested in making it home alive so that they can enjoy their loot. Most of them would never give up their lives to make a million dollars, not to talk of committing suicide for someone or some organization in the name of a deity.

It is because of these cultural factors that the so called experts who think that they understand Nigerians enough to recommend profiling them based on their nationality are simply wrong and wasting their time and resources as the Nigerian lacks the courage to hold ideological or religious beliefs at the expense of his or her own life. To put it simply, a Nigerian could cause others harm as long as it does not affect him personally. And to blow up a plane with the person as one of the victims is definitely un-Nigerian. You can accuse a Nigerian of being too aggressive but not when his or her life is in danger. For most Nigerians, the minute any activity becomes life threatening, they back off and find other ways to live with the situation rather than lose their lives.

The truth of the matter is that Mr. Umar Farouk Abdulmutallab may be Nigerian by birth but definitely not Nigerian by orientation because he was not groomed in Nigeria. Most of his indoctrination occurred in Britain, Dubai, and Yemen where he prepared for his suicide mission. That notwithstanding, it was widely reported that the young man's father expressed the possible radicalization of his son to the U.S. Embassy in the Nigerian capital of Abuja, informing them that he was concerned that his son, who had been studying in Yemen, was being radicalized by Muslim extremists.

Despite all these facts, some in the West still believe that Umar Farouk Abdulmutallab's deranged attempt to bring down a commercial flight over Detroit in 2009 was proof enough that West Africans are becoming radicalized to the point that West Africans, and Nigerians in particular, needed to be singled out for greater scrutiny.

After the Christmas Day bomb attempt, U.S. President Barack Obama immediately ordered a comprehensive visa policy review and tightened rules for Nigerians, particularly students and those between the ages of twenty and sixty, which is practically the entire Nigerian population that travels to and from the United States. According to the Transportation Security Administration (TSA) directive, "Every individual flying into the U.S. from anywhere in the world traveling from or through nations that are state sponsors of terrorism or other countries of interest will be required to go through enhanced screening."[18]

This TSA requirement applies to four countries that the State Department lists on its website as state sponsors of terrorism: Cuba, Iran, Sudan, and Syria as well as other countries of interest. The other countries of interest (which I will call the "List") to which the rule applies include Afghanistan, Algeria, Iraq, Lebanon, Libya, Nigeria, Pakistan, Saudi Arabia, Somalia, and Yemen.

What is glaringly interesting about the List is that Nigeria is the only West African country listed as a country of interest. And, while all the countries on the List have been proven in the past to be exporters or

---

[18] Transportation Security Administration. "TSA Statement on New Security Measures for International Flights to the U.S." http://www.tsa.gov/press/happenings/010310_statement.shtm, January 3, 2010

sympathizers of terrorism, Nigeria is the only nation on the List that since its existence as an entity has never had any of its citizens attempt a terror attack outside of its borders until Umar Farouk Abdulmutallab. Countries whose citizens are known to conduct terrorist attacks outside their borders were not on the list of countries of interest. For example, in 2003, two British citizens named Assaf Mohammed Hanif and Omar Khan Sharif entered Israel with their British passports and carried out a suicide bomb attack in Israel that killed three people and wounded several others[19]. In July 2005, four British citizens including three that were actually born in Britain were involved in the deadliest suicide attacks in London since World War II, which killed 52 people and injured

---

[19] Chris McGreal, Conal Urquhart and Richard Norton-Taylor. "The British suicide bombers", The Guardian, Wednesday 30 April 2003. http://www.guardian.co.uk/world/2003/may/01/israel5

more than 700 other people[20]. Yet, Britain was not included on this so called list of countries of interest.

While 15 of the 19 hijackers that carried out the September 11, 2001 attack were from Saudi Arabia, the other four came from three other countries – one from Egypt, one from Lebanon and two from the United Arab Emirates (UAE). Not only was an Egyptian among the 9/11 hijackers, Ayman Al-Zawahiri who is Osama Bin Laden's right hand man is also Egyptian. Yet, Egypt and UAE did not make the List.

The truth of the matter is that Nigeria is neither a sympathizer of terrorism nor an exporter of terrorists. Nigerians have no history of international terrorism and yet, the President and his administration would have us believe that one naive, brainwashed Muslim lad

---

[20] Kevin J. Strom, Ph.D. and Joe Eyerman, Ph.D. "Interagency Coordination: Lessons Learned From the 2005 London Train Bombings" NIJ Journal, Issue No 261.

makes a nation an exporter of terrorism to the extent that placing that nation on a special travel watch list is warranted.

The security measures approved by the White House included a thorough body search of all Nigerian visitors to the U.S., mandatory seating of all passengers one hour before arrival, a ban on pillows as well as the carrying of bags or electronic devices on laps, and additional deployments of armed marshals on flights into the country. Those travelling through Amsterdam are to be subjected to the controversial body scanning device that sees through clothing in order to detect explosive devices on the body. Within weeks, the Netherlands introduced the body scanners on all flights bound to the United States and Nigeria followed suit.

---

https://www.ncjrs.gov/pdffiles1/nij/224088.pdf

Almost overnight, the Nigerian traveling public began seeing worsening situations at their airports. For example, passengers in Lagos Nigeria were asked to report more than seven hours ahead of their direct flight to Atlanta USA, creating very long lines and unnecessary hardships and confusion for the travelers. Today, while the number of hours required of passengers to appear for check-in has been reduced to three hours at International Airports in Nigeria, the number of checkpoints including scanning stations that passengers must pass through, all in the name of security searches has doubled. When passengers from Nigeria and other West African countries arrive in the United States, they are also subjected to more thorough interrogation.

While it is expected and prudent for security at airports to be tightened as a result of al Qaeda and recent incidents such as the shoe-bomber and underwear bomber attempts, it seems like security agents have singled out West Africans and Nigerians in particular for more detailed interrogations. It's like the attempt by Umar Farouk Abdulmutallab has raised so many concerns for the American authorities that, coupled with concerns about illegal immigration, ill-feelings have spilled over to the vast majority of Nigerian immigrants and travelers who are law-abiding and with no inclination to terrorism whatsoever.

This book focused on the author and other West African immigrants who came to the United States between 1974 and 2004. Many of them that arrived during that period came in quest for higher education. A lot of them initially came to study with the intention of returning to

their homeland to help in the nation-building of
their countries, but decided to stay back in the
United States for one reason or the other. Some
actually fulfilled their goal of returning home
to take jobs that foreign expatriates used to
have, but then had to leave again because of
corruption, political turmoil and/or persecution
in their home countries. For example, in a
report by the United Nation's Human Development,
in 1993, there were more than 21,000 practicing
Nigerian physicians in the United States at a
time when Nigeria's healthcare system was
severely deficient[21]. Despite that these highly
skilled professionals are a tremendous asset to
the United States, it appears that the
government has made them suspects since the 2009
Christmas Day bombing attempt by a lone Nigerian
Muslim lad.

---

[21] Cited in Soumana Sako, "Brain Drain and Africa's Development: A Reflection," *African Issues*, XXX(1), 2002, p. 26.

While profiling is a legitimate technique for deciding how to allocate security resources, catching terrorists through profiling is not effective as terrorists quickly learn new ways to circumvent the system. Instead of wasting scarce resources on profiling, it will be more effective to have every passenger (with sensible deference to senior citizens on wheel chair and children under 8 years old) pass through the body scanning machine if the machines can be made to show less revealing images of people. The screening machines will simply identify any area of the body that has hidden objects and only people that the system raised alerts for, will be further searched or patted down. This approach guarantees that nobody can be discriminated against and no terrorist can slip through the screening system due to profiling.

It seems that the United States has become
a nation consumed by fear, cynicism and
pessimism. The numbers speak for themselves.
Between 1990 and 2000, people born in West
African countries accounted for most of the
African-born immigrants to the United States.
The number of African-born immigrants to the US
increased by 214,941 (192.7 percent), between
that period[22]. Since September 11, 2001, the
number has shrunk immensely spawned in part by
the United States' involvement in Afghanistan
and Iraq. The 9/11 attack and the resulting wars
have undermined what was previously a growing
open and expansive US policy towards West
African immigration.

In many respects, the US immigration policy
appears to have multiple personality problems,
lacking a clear sense of the US priorities and

---

[22] US Census Bureau, Census 2000 and Gibson, Campbell and Emily Lennon, US Census Bureau, Working Paper No. 29, "Historical Census Statistics on the Foreign-Born Population in the United States: 1850 to

values. There is no question that the United

States must have a strong immigration

enforcement strategy that focuses on national

security and restoring integrity to the

immigration laws currently on the books. But we

cannot achieve this through over reaction or

relying too much on enforcement alone. Without a

meaningful consideration for other sensible

immigration reforms, to include a more welcoming

stance, United States risks projecting an image

of an unwelcoming nation – which could be

another tragic outcome of the 9/11 era at the

long run.

1990."

Acknowledgements

I made the decision to write this book entirely myself without the benefit of a ghost writer, but it would not have been possible without the help of some important people. I am especially grateful to the West African immigrants who responded to my survey and shared their stories with me. By sharing their stories, they provided even more insight into just how courageous and determined immigrants are. Although I could not mention their actual names for the purpose of protecting their real identities, the various stories I received made it possible for me to present a better sample of immigrant stories from West Africa and I thank them from the bottom of my heart.

It was such a delight working with the superb team of WordsRU, especially Chief Editor

Jeanmarie who provided lots of insightful comments and suggestions.

I am so grateful to my wife Francisca for all her support, patience and constructive criticisms that I don't have enough words to express my gratitude. As a trained software engineer, I still write software for my business in the evenings when I get home from work and anybody that understands what goes into software development knows how much time software engineers spend sitting in front of a computer. Not only does she put up with my lengthy hours staying up late, but in the last four to five years she has had to sacrifice additional quality time from me because of my writing of this book. I can only say what a gift she gave me the day she became my wife. She is the reason for sweet yesterdays and my promise for tomorrow.

I also want to express my gratitude to my children Brian, Allen, Jaine and Denzel for their inspiration. No matter how rough things get they always manage to remind me about the most important things in life - family.

My thanks also go to my father, Chief Christian Onwezi Nwugwo for reviewing the early version of the manuscript. To everybody who helped in every little measure to make this book a reality, I am deeply grateful. Thank you all.

BC

About the Author

Boniface Chibuzo Nwugwo was born on February 16, 1960 at Alaenyi Ogwa, in the Mbaitoli Local Government Area of Imo State (part of what was the Eastern Region) of Nigeria. Popularly known as B.C. (as his parents refer to their children by their initials), he is the third of nine children born to Juliana and Christian Onwezi Nwugwo. His father, a retired elementary school headmaster, and his mother, a retired seamstress, live part-time in the United States, and part-time in Nigeria.

Boniface is the President and Chief Technical Officer of BTC Technologies LLC, an information technology consulting firm that he founded in 2005. He has over twenty-five years of experience in the software business, having worked for Eastman Kodak Company for sixteen of those years in various technical and leadership capacities, and four years as programmer/analyst for Merkel-Donohue, Inc., a Rochester, New York-based office equipment and design company.

Boniface is a graduate of the State University
of New York, Brockport, where he earned a
Bachelor of Science degree in computer science
and a Master of Public Administration in
information management systems. He earned a
Master of Science in software development &
management from Rochester Institute of
Technology, New York and a PhD in information
technology management from Capella University,
Minneapolis/St Paul Minnesota. He is a senior
member of IEEE and the IEEE Computer Society and
a former Chair of the IEEE Computer Society,
Baltimore Chapter.

Dr. Nwugwo is married, with four children, and
lives in Maryland with his family. He can be
reached at bnwugwo@ieee.org or
bcn@btctechnologies.com.

Index

Lightning Source UK Ltd.
Milton Keynes UK
UKOW03f0626300514

232586UK00001B/24/P